CW00420116

Crossway Bible Guide

Series editors: Ian Coffey (NT), Stephen Gaukroger (OT)
New Testament editor: Steve Motyer

Titles in this series

Ruth and Esther:
Crossway Bible Guide

Debra Reid

Crossway Books Leicester

CROSSWAY BOOKS
38 De Montfort Street, Leicester LE1 7GP, England

First published 2000

British Library Cataloguing in Publication Data
A catalogue record for this book is available from the British Library.

ISBN 1–85684–199–5

Set in Palatino

Typeset in Great Britain

Printed in Great Britain by Omnia Books Ltd, Glasgow

For our parents
Bill and Shirley Harvey and John and Veronica Reid
and for Alun and Alyson:
'May the Lord repay you for what you have done.'
(Ruth 2:12)

CONTENTS

Six routes through Ruth and Esther

Welcome!

These days, meeting together to study the Bible in groups appears to be a booming leisure-time activity in many parts of the world. In the United Kingdom alone, it is estimated that over one million people each week meet in home Bible-study groups.

This series has been designed to help such groups and, in particular, those who lead them. These Bible Guides are also very suitable for individual study, and may help hard-pressed preachers, teachers and students too (see 'How to use this Bible Guide').

We have therefore enlisted authors who are in the business of teaching the Bible to others and are doing it well. They have kept in their sights two clear aims:

1. To explain and apply the message of the Bible in non-technical language.
2. To encourage discussion, prayer and action on what the Bible teaches.

All of us engaged in the project believe that the Bible is the Word of God – given to us in order that people might discover him and his purposes for our lives. We believe that the sixty-six books which go to make up the Bible, although written by different people, in different places, at different times, through different circumstances, have a single unifying theme: that theme is Salvation. This means free forgiveness and the removal of all our guilt, it means the gift of eternal life, and it means the wholeness of purpose and joy which God has designed us to experience here and now, all of this being made possible through the Lord Jesus Christ.

How to use this Bible Guide

These guides have been prepared both for personal study and for the leaders and members of small groups. More information about group study follows on the next few pages.

You can use this book very profitably as a personal study guide. The short studies are ideal for daily reading: the first of the questions provided is usually aimed to help you with personal reflection (see 'How to tackle personal Bible study'). If you prefer to settle down to a longer period of study, you can use groups of three to five studies, and thus get a better overview of a longer Bible passage. In either case, using the Bible Guide will help you to be disciplined about regular study, a habit that countless Christians have found greatly beneficial. (See also 'Six routes through Ruth and Esther' for methods of selecting studies if you do not intend to use them all.)

Yet a third use for these Bible Guides is as a quarry for ideas for the busy Bible teacher, providing outlines and application for those giving talks or sermons or teaching children. You will need more than this book can offer, of course, but the way the Bible text is broken down, comments offered and questions raised may well suggest directions to follow.

How to tackle personal Bible study

We have already suggested that you might use this book as a personal study guide. Now for some more detail.

One of the best methods of Bible study is to read the text through carefully several times, possibly using different versions or translations. Having reflected on the material, it is a good discipline to write down your own thoughts before doing anything else. At this stage it can be useful to consult another background book. See 'Resources' on page 17 and 'For further reading' on page 157. If you are using this book as your main study resource, then read through the relevant sections carefully, turning up the Bible references that are mentioned. The questions at the end of each chapter are specifically designed to help you to apply the passage to your own situation. You may find it helpful to write your answers to the questions in your notes.

It is a good habit to conclude with prayer, bringing before God the things you have learned.

If this kind of in-depth study is too demanding for you and you have only a short time at your disposal, read the Bible passage, read the comments in the Bible Guide, think around one of the questions and commit what you have learned to God in a brief prayer. This would take about fifteen minutes without rushing it.

How to tackle your group Bible study

1. Getting help

If you are new to leading groups, you will obviously want to get all the help you can from ministers and experienced friends. Books are also extremely helpful and we strongly recommend a book prepared by the editors of this series of Bible Guides: *Housegroups: The Leaders' Survival Guide*, edited by Ian Coffey and Stephen Gaukroger (Crossway Books, 1996). This book looks at the whole range of different types of group, asking what is the point of it all, what makes a good leader, how to tackle your meeting, how to help the members, how to study, pray, share and worship, and plenty of other pointers, tips and guidelines.

This book is a 'must' for all leaders of small groups. It is written by a team of people widely experienced in this area. It is available at your local Christian bookshop. If you have difficulty in obtaining a copy, write to Crossway Books, Norton Street, Nottingham NG7 3HR, UK.

2. Planning a programme with your Bible Guide

This guide is a commentary on God's Word, written to help group members to get the most out of their studies. Although it is never ideal to chop up Scripture into small pieces, which its authors never intended, huge chunks are indigestible and we have tried to provide a diet of bite-sized mouthfuls.

This book is divided into major parts, each with a title indicated by a part-title page with a large number. If you want to get an overview of these two Bible books in a series of meetings, you will need to select appropriate studies for each meeting. Read them yourself first and prepare a short summary of the studies you are tackling for your group. Ideally you could write it on a sheet of A5 paper and hand a copy to each member.

Then choose one study from the part you are dealing with as a basis for your meeting. Do not attempt to pack more than one study into one meeting, but choose the crucial one, the study which best crystallizes the message.

If you do not intend to cover the whole Bible text, choose a series of studies to suit the number of meetings you have available. Each part of the commentary is divided into a few (usually three to five) studies. It is a good idea to use consecutive studies, not to dodge about. You will then build up a detailed picture of one section of Scripture. Alternatively, there are six suggested routes through Ruth and Esther on page 11.

3. Resources

You will find any or all of these books of great value in providing background to your Bible knowledge. Put some of them on your Christmas list and build up your library.

New Bible Dictionary or *New Concise Bible Dictionary* (IVP)
New Bible Atlas (IVP)
New Bible Commentary (21st Century edition) (IVP)
Handbook of Life in Bible Times by John Thompson (IVP)
The Bible User's Manual (IVP)

The Lion Handbook to the Bible (Lion Publishing)
The Message of the Bible (Lion Publishing)
NIV Study Bible (Hodder and Stoughton)
The Bible with Pleasure by Steve Motyer (Crossway Books)

The relevant volumes in the IVP Tyndale Commentary series will give you reliable and detailed help with any knotty points you may encounter.

4. Preparing to lead

Reading, discussing with friends, studying, praying, reflecting on life … preparation can be endless. But do not be daunted by that. If you wait to become the perfect leader you will never start at all. The really vital elements in preparation are:

▶ prayer (not only in words but an attitude of dependence on God: 'Lord, I can't manage this on my own')

▶ familiarity with the study passage (careful reading of the text, the Bible Guide study and any other resource books that throw light on it) and

▶ a clear idea of where you hope to get in the meeting (notes on your introduction, perhaps, recap what was covered at the last meeting, and what direction you hope the questions will take you in – don't force the group to give your answers).

Here is a short checklist for the busy group leader:

Have I prayed about the meeting?
Have I decided exactly what I want to achieve through the meeting?
Have I prepared the material?
Am I clear about the questions that will encourage positive group discussion?
Am I gently encouraging silent members?
Am I, again gently, quietening the chatterers?

Am I willing to admit ignorance?

Am I willing to listen to what the group members say and to value their contributions?

Am I ready not to be dogmatic, not imposing my ideas on the group?

Have I planned how to involve the members in discovering for themselves?

Have I developed several 'prayer points' that will help focus the group?

Are we applying Scripture to our experience of real life or only using it as a peg to hang our opinions on?

Are we finding resources for action and change or just having a nice talk?

Are we all enjoying the experience together?

What can we expect to learn from Ruth and Esther?

God can be trusted even in terrible circumstances

► He provides for our physical, spiritual and emotional needs.

► Coincidences are often 'God-incidents'.

► No-one can thwart God's purposes.

► God's goodness does not end when problems begin.

► Terrible circumstances can reveal God's mercy and our inner resources of faith and character.

God involves his people in his work

► God may choose to call, use and bless even me!

► Being involved in God's work may require courageous faith and action.

► The people God chooses are not perfect but willing.

► Our personal relationships need to mirror God's own character, displaying love, loyalty, lovingkindness and integrity.

19

▶ His people need to celebrate his work.

God is able to change things completely

▶ He often surprises us.

▶ He enables the humble, poor and disadvantaged to become powerful, rich and blessed.

▶ God's honour will ultimately be upheld.

Finding your way around this book

In our Bible Guides we have developed special symbols to make things easier to follow. Every study therefore has an opening section which is the passage in a nutshell.

 The main section is the one that *makes sense of the passage.*

Questions

Every passage also has special questions for personal and group study after the main section. Some questions are addressed to us as individuals, some speak to us as members of our church or home group, while others concern us as members of God's people worldwide. The questions are deliberately designed

▸ to get people thinking about the passage

▸ to apply the text to 'real life' situations

▸ to encourage reflection, discussion and action!

As a group leader you may well discover additional questions that will have special relevance to your group, so look out for these and note them in your preparation time.

Stop and look

This feature gives us the chance to stand back from the action and take stock. It gives a summary of what to look for in the passages we are about to read, and useful background material.

Digging deeper

Some passages, however, require an extra amount of explanation, and we have put these sections into two categories. The first kind gives additional background material that helps us to understand something factual. For example, if we dig deeper into the Gospels, it helps us to know who the Pharisees were, so that we can see more easily why they related to Jesus in the way they did. These technical sections are marked with a spade.

Important doctrines

The second kind of background section appears with passages which have important doctrines contained in them and which we need to study in more depth if we are to grow as Christians. Special sections that explain them to us in greater detail are marked with a face as above.

THE BOOK OF RUTH

Why read the book of Ruth?

Most of us enjoy an intriguing story. The story of Ruth is full of intrigue; we are left to puzzle out many of its details. It also is an unusual story within the Old Testament, focusing as it does upon the troubles and subsequent joys of one particular family unit. The experiences of this family arise within a social context which is very different from our own. Even so, we can't read Ruth's story without being challenged by its message and theme.

The story is well written, easy to read and refreshingly simple. It tells of the fortunes of a woman called Naomi and her family. It has an unhappy beginning, an uncertain middle and a happy ending. It is set in the context of Israel's journey of faith. But the book of Ruth is more than a good story. We discover that God's purposes are at work even in the lives of his 'ordinary' people. Understanding those purposes is vital to our knowledge of him and our grasp of what he wants to do in us. Ruth's story tells us loud and clear that through the ordinary and unpredictable aspects of everyday life, we can experience the reality of God's care. But the writer of Ruth's story does not impose this theological emphasis on the story. Instead, God's role is acknowledged by the characters themselves, who show clearly that they recognize that God is at work as their own life stories unfold.

The author of the book is unknown, but may have been a woman. The story is told from a female point of view and certainly seems to commend Naomi and Ruth to us. Their determination and assertiveness are vital to the story. These women show remarkable levels of selfless devotion and care for each other, and this leads each of them to take risks for the other's sake. In hardship, insecurity and bereavement Ruth and Naomi try to transform their circumstances. They are interested not only in survival but in changing things completely. For women in Old Testament times, husband and home were synonymous with a sense of identity, security and worth. Naomi and Ruth are without both when we meet them at the start of their story. At the story's conclusion, however, their identity, security and worth are beyond doubt. This explains the incredulous joy that punctuates the story towards its end. Naomi and her family have turned from an empty and bitter void (chapter 1) to new lives of joy and fulfilment (chapter 4). Other female characters also take key roles in the story: it is Naomi's friends who recognize that the Lord himself was ultimately responsible for the transformed circumstances (4:14). In the hands of another writer it might have been the male friends of Boaz that produced such a comment.

The book of Ruth is set in 'the days when the judges ruled' (the twelfth or eleventh century BC; Ruth 1:1). It is usually suggested that the story was written during the early years of the monarchy (the tenth century BC). The judges ruled during a time of religious uncertainty which was also marked by a serious conflict between the Israelites and Moab (Judges 3:12–30). The story seems to reflect a time when there was a break in that conflict. It is this historical setting that makes it even more remarkable that Ruth, a Moabite, eventually marries Boaz who is an Israelite. Moreover, this unlikely marriage made Ruth, the Moabite, the great-grandmother of King David. The book of Ruth helps to set the background for the great achievements of this famous Israelite king. God chose to bless and use David in a special way in the unfolding story of Israel's history and faith, and Ruth is part of that story.

The main reason for writing down the story of Ruth may have been to show how God was at work in David's ancestry. Some people have thought that the story was intended to counter the rejection of mixed marriages which is prominent in the books of Ezra and Nehemiah. Certainly Ruth's faith as a believing Gentile is commended in the story. But Ruth also shows loyalty and lovingkindness, and the story seems to promote these virtues as well.

Whatever its original purpose, this Old Testament book is a direct challenge to prejudice, whether chauvinism or nationalism. It extols the value of loyalty and kindness in personal, business and social relationships. Whatever our gender, race or circumstances, it commends to us faith in the security of God's providential care for ordinary people. Such faith may demand risks. But for Naomi and Ruth, risk-taking means that tragedy and desperation are replaced by hope and security.

GOD IS IN CONTROL

Ruth 1

Stop and look

Is God really in control of our lives and our circumstances? Can we be certain that he is involved in our lives even when their every aspect seems dark and difficult? 'Yes!' comes the resounding answer in the books of Ruth and Esther. These books are not alone in this. The assurance is there throughout Scripture. In the ups and downs of their early history, the people of Israel discover that God works on their behalf even when they endure the horrors of slavery and homelessness. Facing impossible military battles and hostile nations, they learn that God hears their cry and acts to relieve their difficulties. Individuals struggle with their faith in testing times, and yet somehow their strength and trust enable them to make powerful statements of faith: think of many of the Psalms or the story of Job. In fact, Job's story has many parallels with the story of Ruth. Job's family, like Naomi's, suddenly finds itself in dire circumstances. But amid those circumstances both Job and Naomi discover a deep faith in their God. Job declares, 'I know that my Redeemer lives' (Job 19:25). Naomi's friends say to her, 'Praise be to the LORD, who this day has not left you without a kinsman-redeemer' (Ruth 4:14). Both stories show that we can affirm God's control and influence over our lives even in the difficult times.

Ruth 1 hints at this theme throughout. Verse 6 affirms that God provides for the physical needs of his people. Verses 8–9 bear witness to Naomi's belief that the Lord shows kindness and gives rest to his people (and that Naomi can trust her family to God's care wherever they go). But her struggle of faith is evident when she says that the bad things that have happened to her are from the Lord's hand (verses 13, 20–21). The fact that God is in control does not save us from difficulties, but it gives us hope and strength as we endure such trials (see James 1:2–3).

Naomi's tragedy, faith and friendship

After experiencing personal tragedy Naomi returns to her homeland with Ruth, her devoted daughter-in-law.

The book of Ruth is full of contrasts, and this opening chapter is no exception.

▶ The despair of bereavement contrasts with the comfort of loyal friendship.

▶ The recognition that the Lord brings difficulties (verse 21) contrasts with the belief that he shows kindness (verse 8).

▶ The leaving of homeland, first by Naomi (verse 1) and then by Ruth (verses 16–19), contrasts with Naomi's return to homeland (verse 22).

These contrasts set the scene for the story as it unfolds. The contrasts focus on the dire personal circumstances which this ordinary family faces. Even so, we can see that the lives of the family members are in the Lord's hands. This is shown by the contrasting features of the opening and concluding verses:

▶ the leaving is replaced by the hope in returning;

▶ the famine is replaced by the beginning of the barley harvest;

▶ the void of bereavements is filled by a new depth of relationship between Ruth and Naomi.

In this study we shall look at these events from Naomi's point of view.

Verses 1–5 set a tragic scene. Naomi finds herself in a foreign and potentially hostile place. She is widowed (verse 3) and then further bereaved by the death of her two sons (verse 5). We cannot miss the devastating nature of her losses. It seems that within a period of ten years (verse 4) Naomi's complete immediate family is taken away from her. In Old Testament times a widow's position was thought of in the same way as that of orphans and foreigners, as widows were insecure and vulnerable. While in Moab, of course, Naomi was a foreigner too. She was without provision, protection and prospects. It is not surprising that she felt keenly the bitter pain of her experiences (verses 20–21).

But Naomi is also a woman of faith. The writer makes this point strongly.

▶ Naomi is alert to the Lord's work in her life and homeland. She 'heard ... that the LORD had come to the aid of his people' (verse 6), and she acts on this knowledge by preparing to return to Bethlehem (verse 7).

▶ She prays for her two daughters-in-law. She wants their future to be marked by God's kindness and human kindness in the shape of new husbands (verses 8–9).

There is something remarkably unselfish and trusting about Naomi's words. She is concerned with Ruth's and Orpah's welfare, not her own. She expresses confidence that the God of kindness would reward the kindness of her daughters-in-law by his blessing. Of course, the irony is that as Naomi expresses her own kindness to Ruth and Orpah, she herself journeys into God's rewarding kindness (which becomes reality at the end of chapter 4).

But Ruth is determined to stay with Naomi (verses 11–18). This is perhaps a mark of the love and respect that

Naomi had earned from her daughter-in-law. By heeding Ruth's determination (verse 18), Naomi shows that this respect is mutual.

As Naomi shares her family news with the women from her home town, realism and faith combine. Verses 20–21 are littered with graphic words of suffering ('bitter', 'empty', 'afflicted', 'misfortune'). Naomi does not play down the reality of her pain. But it is interesting that she uses the name 'Shaddai' (Almighty) for God. This suggests that she recognizes that though God is responsible for the disasters, he is still in charge of her life. The name 'Shaddai' is often used in connection with God's powerful hand of deliverance or judgment. It expresses belief that God's work is beyond human scrutiny and explanation, and Naomi seems to accept this.

In this chapter, Naomi's character is carefully described to us. She has not collapsed under her painful experiences; her resolve is secure and her faith remains intact. In this sense her adversity has shown her and us what she is made of, but it has also introduced her afresh to her God.

Questions

1. Think back to a bereavement or tragedy you have suffered. How did you respond? Why did you respond in that way? What do you feel about that time in your life now? If you were able to bring your need to God, what difference did it make?

2. In church life (as well as in family life), we can be so dominated by our own concerns that we neglect the needs of others. Naomi was able to keep these things in balance. Look again at her prayers in verses 8–9, and then convert these words into your own prayers for those you know who have suffered, or who have been kind to you.

3. Who are the disadvantaged in our society, and what can society do to improve their lot? What practical part can you play?

Character names

The story of Ruth is carefully designed. As part of this design the names which appear in the text are significant.

In chapter 1 we are introduced to Elimelech (meaning 'my god is king') which may stand in parallel to Naomi's use of the name 'Shaddai' (Almighty) to describe the Lord. The meaning of the title 'Shaddai' is not entirely clear although it occurs frequently in the Old Testament to emphasize the power of God (see e.g. Isaiah 13:6; Joel 1:15). The title is used to emphasize God's power to bless (e.g. Genesis 28:3; 35:11), to protect (Psalm 91:1–2) and to discipline (Job 5:17). By using the name 'Shaddai', Naomi is recognizing that God's power is the determining factor in her life. His work cannot be resisted, but must be accepted, as her present circumstances indicate.

The name 'Naomi' (meaning 'pleasant' or 'beautiful') is ironic because her early experiences are anything but pleasant (as her request to be called Mara, 'bitter', affirms).

Among eastern people names were commonly changed when momentous events occurred in their lives. In the Bible we see plenty of evidence for this. In Genesis, for example, we read about Abram's name being changed to Abraham (Genesis 17:5) and Sarai's name being changed to Sarah (Genesis 17:15). Similarly, Jacob becomes known as Israel to commemorate his prayer (Genesis 32:28; 35:10) and Joseph is named Zaphenath-Paneah in recognition of his ability to reveal secrets (Genesis 41:45). Other examples of name-changing occur throughout the Old Testament text.

While Naomi's sons' names are Canaanite in origin (generally thought to be derived from words denoting illness or weakness), 'Ruth' and 'Orpah' are Moabite names. Their meaning is uncertain, although there have been attempts to connect them with the Hebrew words meaning 'comfort' and 'turning back'.

The author of the book of Ruth is primarily interested in the meaning of the name 'Naomi', which is pivotal as the story progresses. Naomi's life moves her through the cycle of pleasantness–bitterness–pleasantness that dominates the story's development.

Ruth 1:1–22

Ruth's tragedy, faith and friendship

Ruth throws in her lot with Naomi, her people and her God.

 I recently attended a silver-wedding celebration. It was a lovely occasion, with good company, pleasant surroundings and great food. But the most memorable moment was a short speech by the husband, who commented that he and his wife were grateful for many good times and hoped that the difficult times had made them 'better, not bitter', people. I immediately thought about the life of Ruth, the young woman whose character and faith seem to have been refined in her difficult times.

Because Naomi is the focus of the story during chapter 1, it is easy to miss Ruth's own tragedy. Admittedly, Naomi had lost her husband and two sons, but Ruth too had lost her husband, and presumably there had been no children. They had been married for no more than ten years (verses 4–5). As women with no husband, father-in-law, brother-in-law or son, Ruth and Orpah faced, with Naomi, an uncertain and insecure future. Naomi's words to her daughters-in-law (verses 8–13) suggest that their best chance was to forget the unfortunate family they had married into, and begin afresh in their homeland. The writer does not condemn Orpah for adopting this sensible path (verse 14). Orpah's love for Naomi is not questioned. She makes a difficult decision, and accepts Naomi's advice. The quality of Ruth's relationship with Naomi is different, and it leads her to make a different decision.

As Orpah leaves Naomi, Ruth clings to her (verse 14). This is a strong verb which is also used in Genesis 2:24 to explain the relationship established between a man and his wife when the man leaves his mother and father. This verb suggests a relationship that is binding, all-encompassing and exclusive. It rules out the possibility of future abandonment. It has its focus in the future rather than in the past. The same verb is used in Deuteronomy 10:20 in the command to Israel to fear and serve the Lord. God's people are instructed to cling or 'hold fast' to him and take oaths in his name. This is exactly what Ruth does in the verses that follow. By using this word in verse 14, the writer prepares us for the young Moabite woman's clear declaration of loyalty expressed in the language of oath or covenant in verses 16–17. Ruth's words are both a promise and a statement. They are bold and profound, but also simple and trusting.

They express devotion at three levels:

► devotion to Naomi herself;

► devotion and commitment to Naomi's nation;

► devotion to Naomi's God.

Ruth also makes it clear that this decision is not just for the moment but for life (verse 17). Her pledge is serious. It is underlined by the oath-like conclusion: 'may the LORD deal with me, be it ever so severely'. Although Naomi wanted to protect Ruth's interests, she didn't try to counter convictions this strong.

Verses 16–17 are the climax of the chapter. The desperation of the early verses is balanced by the hope which this level of devotion always allows. It is devotion that justifies Ruth's choice to abandon good sense. Her heart rules her head, but we don't criticize her for it. Her own tragedy has established a faith and a loyalty which are motivated by love and conviction. She keeps faith with Naomi and this in turn reflects her deep faith in God. In her difficult times, Ruth has become not bitter but better, and this legitimizes her advance into centre stage as this chapter concludes and the story progresses.

Questions

1. Put yourself in Ruth's shoes. Would you have stayed with Naomi? If not, what reasons could you have given to justify your actions?
2. Try writing down a covenant (or words of promise) between yourself and either a friend or member of your study group or church. Make your promise as practical as possible, and don't forget to make it reflect both your faith in God and your loving concern for your friend. You could begin with the words, 'Because God has shown his selfless love for me, I want to show my love for you. I will do this by … '
   In what ways does your promise reflect Ruth's words? In what ways does it differ?
3. Ruth is prepared to live in a foreign land away from her natural family. How would you feel if you thought God was calling you to do the same?

Covenant love

The word 'kindness' (1:8) translates the Hebrew *ḥesed*, and represents a central theme in the book of Ruth. Within the Old Testament it describes the nature of God's relationship to Israel. It means committed, loyal love, often expressed through a covenant relationship – a formal, guaranteed agreement. It is a deliberate, lasting and consistent relationship that does not depend on circumstance or merit. God shows covenant love to his people (Deuteronomy 7:7–9), and they are called to respond with loving devotion (see e.g. Deuteronomy 10:12–22). In the book that bears her name, Ruth's kindness is commended (3:10) and God's kindness is acknowledged (2:20). In this way Ruth reflects God's own character and purposes. She exemplifies the loyalty God looks for in his people, even though she is a Moabite. So Ruth has a role to play in God's unfolding covenant purposes for Israel as her story progresses.

GOD PROVIDES REFUGE

Ruth 2:1 – 3:5

Stop and look

Many Christians are familiar with verses in the Bible which speak of God as our refuge. Perhaps the most famous verse is Psalm 46:1: 'God is our refuge and strength, an ever-present help in trouble.' This verse summarizes as helpfully as any other the message of the book of Ruth. Ruth discovers that God himself is the one who protects her and defends her cause. The events of her life are 'God-events' because he is always present with her. Boaz voices this theme of God's protection in 2:12. This anticipates and emphasizes the fact that Boaz is to be the instrument that God uses to look after Ruth and Naomi. But Boaz recognizes that God is very much at the centre of this story, as he echoes imagery used elsewhere in the Old Testament. In Deuteronomy 32, Moses compares the shielding and caring work of God to an eagle caring for its young (see especially verses 10–12), and this seems to be similar to Boaz's image of the wings of God providing refuge for Ruth. The idea of refuge encompasses protection, safety, provision, help, hope and refreshment. Throughout the passages brought together in this section, this is the dominant theme. In times of uncertainty and vulnerability Ruth discovers that the God of Israel is her refuge and her God.

Love at first sight?

Ruth meets Boaz and receives unexpected praise and favour from him.

At this point in the story we begin to anticipate a turnaround. The happy ending to the sad story starts here. A hard day's work in the field becomes an occasion for favour and blessing as this 'chance' meeting with Boaz's harvesters takes place.

The writer of the book wants us to see that Ruth and Boaz are like-minded people. The similarities between them are emphasized. Boaz praises Ruth for her kindness to Naomi (verses 11–12) and Ruth praises Boaz for his generous kindness to her (verses 10, 13). As Boaz enters the story he greets his workforce (verse 4). We may have expected a simple 'Shalom' ('Peace', 'Hello'), but instead he calls out, 'The LORD be with you!' This suggests that Boaz is a popular landowner who values his employees. The workers respond, 'The LORD bless you!' Boaz is clearly a good, kind man; a man who is suitable for good, kind Ruth.

But Boaz is also a relative. Just in case we miss this important fact, the author tells us twice that Boaz is 'from the clan of Elimelech' (verses 1, 3). In Israelite society relatives had special responsibilities toward other family members, particularly to those who experienced bereavement or poverty. So Boaz arrives on the scene as a figure of hope and restoration. He apparently does so by chance ('as it turned out', verse 3). The implication is that divine providence is at work. Ruth's choice of field has been determined by the Lord himself. This providence is celebrated by Naomi's friends at the end of the story: 'Praise be to the LORD, who this day has not left you without a kinsman-redeemer' (4:14). Ruth's story is God's story, so it is appropriate to respond to it by praising him.

When Boaz arrives on the scene, his attention is immediately taken up with Ruth (verse 5). Why? Maybe she was particularly attractive. Maybe, as a Moabite, she looked different or dressed differently from the other women. Maybe Boaz noticed how hard she was working. Whatever the reason, Ruth made a good first impression, and Boaz was eager to find out more about her. His question startles us: he doesn't ask, 'Who is that?' but 'Who does she belong to?' His question is ambiguous. Did Boaz want to know who Ruth was working for, or was he really asking whether she was available for marriage? Perhaps the ambiguity is deliberate, for the answer he receives assumes he knows more than he lets on about the circumstances of the Moabite woman who returned with Naomi (verse 6). It seems that news of Ruth has gone before her and Boaz is concerned for her safety and her reputation (verses 8–9). Boaz's favourable response to Ruth is nothing more than she deserves and that we expect. But Ruth herself remains modest and respectful. She behaves perfectly.

► She recognizes that Boaz is worthy of respect; she bows down to him (verse 10) and calls him 'my lord' (verse 13).

► She is grateful for his 'favour' towards her (verses 10, 13 – a word particularly used for the undeserved kindness of a superior to a subordinate).

► She is aware of her precarious position; she is less important than one of Boaz's servant girls (verse 13).

Ruth makes no claim to Boaz's special favour. Instead, her only claim is that Boaz is unduly kind to her. She remains vulnerable, and yet her respect and restraint draw attention to her courage and integrity. Boaz himself picks up on this in verses 11–12.

These verses also emphasize the integrity of Boaz. He

values Ruth's selfless courage in bereavement, expressed in her devotion to Naomi. He commends Ruth to the Lord's hand for blessing and protection. The end of verse 12 is significant, for Boaz says that Ruth has 'come to take refuge' under the wings of Israel's God. The idea of the Lord's protecting wings comes from the image of a bird covering its defenceless young (compare Psalm 91:4). Ruth too is both young and vulnerable. The image confirms that she is a woman of faith and that Boaz accepts her as someone included in the covenant community of Israel, even though she is a Moabite. So Ruth can expect two levels of blessing:

▶ Boaz can show favour toward her, and

▶ her rich 'reward' will come from the Lord himself.

The word 'reward' occurs in Psalm 127:3: 'sons are a heritage from the LORD, children a reward from him.' The writer may be hinting at the joyous conclusion when Ruth and Boaz's first son is born (4:13). Future events are often anticipated in this story.

Ruth's uncertainty and vulnerability are, however, disappearing as Boaz shows her acceptance and favour. We feel eager to see how things will turn out. Naomi's tragedy has not been forgotten, but from here on it remains mainly in the background. Her life will be restored as Ruth's story unfolds.

Questions

1. What first impression do you make when you meet or work with someone for the first time? What reputation goes before you? (If you are studying in a group, try to think back. What can you remember about when you met each other for the first time?)
2. Boaz recognized Ruth's practical faith despite her background and youth. In your church, do you welcome *all* those who belong to God's family? How can you improve matters?

3. What example does Boaz give to employers? What example does Ruth give to the unemployed?

Gleaning

Although the storyline is clear, some of the details in this Old Testament book are obscure to us today. The custom of gleaning is one example. The right of the poor to glean was well established and protected by laws which prevented greedy or unscrupulous landowners undermining these rights (see Leviticus 19:9–10; Deuteronomy 24:19–22). Gleaners were allowed to pick up grain (or fruit) left by the harvesters. The custom of gleaning thus provided a way in which the poor could work for their survival in ancient Palestine.

Deuteronomy 24:19 highlights that gleaning is a provision especially made for widows. Ruth may not have been fully aware of the protection the laws of Israel gave her, and her eagerness to find someone with a field to harvest who would be nice ('favourable', 2:2) is perhaps wisely cautious. It is obvious from our story that for a woman like Ruth gleaning was still a dangerous occupation (2:9, 22), presumably because overseers might be rough with the gleaners or even demand sexual favours. Boaz is keen to protect Ruth from possible abuse (verses 15–16). Boaz's workers would, after all, have known that their own rights and responsibilities as reapers superseded those of the gleaners. The boundary between reaping and gleaning had to be protected. Tensions were always possible – especially as Ruth followed directly behind the servant girls (verses 8–9). She was in a privileged position, guaranteeing her good success.

Ruth 2:14–18

More than plenty

Boaz invites Ruth to a meal and arranges for her day's work to be astonishingly successful.

Boaz's generosity to Ruth extends even further. He heaps one kindness upon another. He grants her privileges that will have stunned his harvesters as they  witnessed all that happens. There is irony in the fact that at this stage Ruth does not know that Boaz is Naomi's relative. She is surprised by his response to her. But we are not surprised, because the writer has ensured that we know about Boaz's family background (verses 1, 3). We have already started to think that Boaz will respond positively to Ruth.

But these verses do more than point out Boaz's generous nature. They bring Naomi's fortunes back into view. Naomi advises Ruth to stay in Boaz's field (verse 22) and orchestrates the rather risky meeting between Ruth and Boaz in chapter 3. Here Naomi's fortunes begin to turn round from bitterness to joy. A contrast is drawn between her previous emptiness (1:21) and the plenty which she and Ruth can now enjoy (2:18).

Boaz acts

Verses 14–18 illustrate how Boaz goes beyond the normal bounds of generosity and exceeds all expectations. First, he invites Ruth to share a meal with his harvesters. This is astonishing. Ruth herself has just admitted that she is less important than even one of his young servant girls (verse 13), and now she is permitted to sit beside the harvesters. It appears that Boaz even serves Ruth, offering the roasted grain (verse 14). This may have been a delicacy of some sort which was accompanied by the more basic and traditional elements of such meals (bread and wine vinegar). The details of the meal are passed over quite quickly. The important fact is summarized in the phrase, 'She ate all she wanted and had some left over.' The meal shows three things:

▶ Ruth is integrated with Boaz's working household;

▶ Boaz is a most generous man;

▶ Boaz has given Ruth more than refreshment, rest and food; he has given her respect.

Boaz's favours to Ruth continue (verses 15–16). He tells his harvesters to allow her to glean among the sheaves (not just on the field edge, as the law required), and instructs them to pull out grain from their bundles deliberately, so that she can pick it up. Boaz is meticulous in making all the arrangements. He doesn't want Ruth to be put off by practical difficulties or by what his young men might say. This is an important point. Boaz recognizes the power of spoken words, so he instructs his young men accordingly. We do well to recognize too that our words, as much as our actions, are capable of undoing another person (compare James 1:19; 3:1–12).

Ruth responds

Ruth plays her own part too. She still works a long day, not stopping until evening, after which she has to thresh the barley and carry it home (verses 17–18). It is perhaps surprising that Boaz didn't intervene even further to help Ruth with these tasks. But the writer of this story is trying to describe Ruth's industry and exemplary character as well as indicating Boaz's generosity. The amount of threshed barley was 'about an ephah'. The exact measure this represents is unclear and in any case is not important. It far exceeds the expectation for a gleaner's day's work, while still being an amount Ruth could manage to carry. (The description suggests something similar to a woman struggling home from the supermarket with six bags of shopping.) Ruth, thanks to Boaz, staggers home to Naomi not just with the result of her day's work but also with the remains of the meal she enjoyed with Boaz. Again Ruth's devotion to Naomi is evident from her concern for Naomi's physical needs. As we are reminded of Naomi's own needs, the stage is set for both women to share their overwhelming joy. We eagerly anticipate that more is to come in this great reversal of fortunes. The two women who had arrived empty-handed, but in time for harvest, have food – probably enough for several weeks. Their immediate need for physical provision has been met.

Questions

1. What would the other gleaners have said to each other as they witnessed the day's events? If you are studying in a group, why not act out the scene for yourselves?
2. Boaz's servants co-operated with him in his plans for Ruth. As members of churches, how well do we go along with our leaders and become partners in their vision? What challenges does this present to us?
3. Boaz went beyond the call of duty in providing generously for Ruth. In what ways are we called today to respond to the needs of others in our world? What does our response indicate about our relationship with God?

Ruth 2:19–23

Family ties

Naomi encourages Ruth to stay in Boaz's field until the end of harvest. With joy she recognizes the Lord's kindness.

 The working pattern of police officers and detectives involves frequent de-briefing sessions. At the end of a shift's operations a team of detectives will sit down and evaluate the progress they have made. Successes are noted, difficulties are evaluated, different views are aired and the next stage is planned. The conclusions will influence the team's work and dictate its operations in subsequent days, months and even years.

In the verses which conclude this second chapter, Naomi and Ruth now evaluate the day's events. Their responses, and the decisions they take, will determine the path of their future lives.

Joy

Naomi and Ruth agree that the day has been a success. You can almost see the excitement on their faces as they acknowledge how generous Boaz has been (verses 20–21). Naomi suggests that Ruth should stay in Boaz's field (verse 22), and it is clear from Ruth's actions that she concurs with this advice (verse 23). Of course, there is no reason why Ruth shouldn't agree; the evidence of the day's events suggests this is a sensible move. The details of this 'debrief' are therefore straightforward, but the way the writer records this conversation between Ruth and her mother-in-law intrigues us.

Verse 19 begins with two parallel questions from Naomi,

which give way immediately to words in praise of the anonymous 'man' who has taken notice of Ruth. Naomi's excitement seems to bubble over so much that she doesn't even wait for her questions to be answered before she utters words of blessing on whoever has treated Ruth with such respect and kindness. The second half of the verse creates suspense as the writer slows down the pace with an explanatory sentence before Ruth finally declares that the man is Boaz. At this news Naomi's excitement gives way to unbridled joy as she restates her blessing (verse 20). The words 'He has not stopped showing his kindness' may refer either to the Lord or to Boaz. The ambiguity may be deliberate, for Boaz now becomes the vehicle of God's kindness (as recognized by Naomi's friends in 4:14). If Boaz is the intended subject (which would after all take up the emphasis in Ruth's statement at the end of verse 19), then a further parallel is made between Ruth and Boaz: they both benefit from Naomi's prayer for blessing (compare 1:8; 2:20). In both prayers these people are commended because they show kindness to those living as well as to the dead. In 2:20 this implies that the whole family, past and present, benefits from such kindness (*ḥesed*). As those who show *ḥesed*, Ruth and Boaz live out the ideals associated with being God's covenant people. (Compare Micah 6:8, where to love mercy, or kindness, is central to our duty to God.)

Hope

Naomi tells Ruth that Boaz is a 'close relative' and 'one of our kinsman-redeemers' (2:20). These terms have overtones of hope and promise. 'Kinsman-redeemer' (the Hebrew word is *gōʾēl*) is the title given to someone who redeems or protects the rights of another family member. By using the pronoun 'our', it is clear that Naomi views Ruth as part of her intimate family. She is entitled to the protection and redemption that the *gōʾēl* brings. It is somewhat surprising, then, that the writer quickly reminds us of Ruth's foreign status as a Moabite (verse 21). This must serve to emphasize again that Boaz's kindness was unexpected as well as generous. The effect of his favours was to last for a while. Harvest-time would normally extend for about two months. If Ruth's first day's gleaning is anything to go by, she would glean enough to provide Naomi and herself with food for a whole year. She remains in Boaz's field. This would presumably lead to further meetings with him, so our expectations are high concerning what may develop.

The chapter ends with some mother-to-daughter advice (verse 22) which Ruth follows carefully (verse 23). Naomi instructs Ruth to 'go with his girls' (verse 22), which contrasts with Ruth's word 'workers' (verse 21). The point is that Naomi is keen to protect Ruth from accusation and harm. Ruth would be wise, therefore, to attach herself to Boaz's female employees, rather than to his male ones. The chapter ends by stating that Ruth 'lived with her mother-in-law'. Their commitment to each other remains intact, but we anticipate a future that will reap the consequences of Boaz's kindness and God's provision for these deserving women.

Questions

1. What can we learn from the relationship between Ruth and Naomi in these verses? How should we reflect their example? What are our responsibilities for the welfare of our in-laws, and how can we fulfil them?
2. Boaz reflects God's own character and standard of lovingkindness. What does it mean in church life to act as God to each other?
3. Our actions can easily be misunderstood, and this could lead to unnecessary harm. Can you think of any modern-day equivalents to 'staying close to his girls'? Why are reputations important, for both men and women?

The gō'ēl

This is the Hebrew word translated 'kinsman-redeemer'. The *gō'ēl* was usually the closest male relative, and he was expected to come to the rescue in the event of severe hardship or misfortune. He was to redeem land or people if, on account of poverty, a family member was forced to sell land, or even to sell himself or herself into slavery. He was also responsible for avenging murder, and for organizing restitution in other cases of wrongdoing. In other words, the *gō'ēl's* duty was to protect a family member in dire straits. In Old Testament times this obligation extended to providing sons for childless widows within the family circle. In the story of Ruth the important point is that Mahlon, Ruth's husband, had died before children had been conceived. The responsibility therefore falls upon the nearest kinsman to marry the widow and provide a child to carry on Mahlon's name (see Deuteronomy 25:5–10). There is also a responsibility to rescue the land Naomi is selling so that it doesn't pass outside the family (see Leviticus 25:25). The role of *gō'ēl* depended strongly upon a sense of family loyalty and upholding family honour. (See 'Levirate marriage', pp. 67–68.) The fact that fathering children is part of the responsibility gives Boaz the opportunity to step in as kinsman-redeemer (rather than the closer relative, 4:5–6).

So the *gō'ēl* played an important role in the system of family responsibility and loyalty within Israel's community life. The specific tasks belonging to the *gō'ēl* reflect the Lord's own work in redeeming, restoring and protecting Israel. In their family relationships God's people are to imitate God's own character and his commitment to them. The divine work of redemption is carried forward in the story of Ruth by the birth of her son, Obed, the grandfather of King David. Through David, the Lord's redeeming, restoring and protecting activity is made visible. From

David's line comes Jesus who, in his life, death, resurrection and ascension, redeemed the world for God.

Ruth 3:1–5

Mother-in-law knows best!

Naomi sends Ruth to meet Boaz on the threshing-floor. She receives Ruth's report on the encounter.

How do you react to mother-in-law jokes? I don't engage with them at all. I have a superb mother-in-law. She child-minds, irons, cleans, does the gardening, cries with me and laughs with me. She's always there when she's needed. In fact, there's nothing that she wouldn't do for me – except perhaps scheme as openly as Naomi does in these verses!

Naomi could be accused of blatant interference, but that's not the way Ruth interprets her mother-in-law's advice. Ruth simply but definitely agrees to do as Naomi suggests (verse 5). Following advice is a mark of personal humility, and also indicates loving and trusting respect. We would do well to follow Ruth's example by humbly following advice when it is given by someone (perhaps older and wiser than we are) who has our best interests at heart.

Get ready and go!

The close relationship between Ruth and Naomi is obvious. Naomi calls Ruth 'my daughter' (verse 1) and begins to unfold her plan. The relationship legitimizes the advice Naomi gives. We assume that Naomi is confident of Ruth's attractiveness to Boaz and has decided that now is the time to take the initiative. Naomi's determination and assertiveness are again evident. This woman doesn't sit back and let events happen around her; she makes things happen. But Naomi is not driven by self-interest. She is concerned for Ruth's continued well-being and is determined that the insecurity of widowhood will not be her lot for ever (verse 1). It is easy to miss the significance of Naomi's concern for Ruth; she wants Ruth to have a home. We might expect Naomi to be more concerned about an heir for Elimelech, but this is not even mentioned. Naomi does not send Ruth on a guilt trip about her family responsibilities; instead, she herself assumes full responsibility for Ruth's well-being. She has lost sight of her own needs and can therefore concentrate on Ruth's interests.

Naomi has done her research. She knows Boaz will winnow barley at the end of the day when the light evening winds would blow away the chaff but not the grain. She knows that he would then eat and drink before resting (verses 3–4), and she seems certain that he will respond to Ruth in a positive way ('He will tell you what to do,' verse 4). This confidence is based on Boaz's status as 'kinsman' (verse 2) and presumably on the kindness which Boaz continues to show Ruth during the harvesting season (2:23). The instructions given to Ruth (verses 3–4) are clear. She is to get ready and then go to the threshing-floor. Washing, putting on perfume, and getting dressed were part of the routine of getting ready to go out. When all three aspects of this routine are mentioned together it normally means one of two things.

First, the preparations may be for a special occasion, such as when a bride gets ready for her wedding. Indeed, there are parallels with Ezekiel 16:8–12, which uses the metaphor of bride and groom to explain the Lord's relationship to Jerusalem. While washing, putting on perfume, and dressing are mentioned in both passages, the Ezekiel passage has additional features. The bride is clothed in an 'embroidered dress' of 'fine linen', and 'leather sandals', with 'bracelets', 'necklace' and 'ear-rings'.

Alternatively, the preparations may mark the end of a period of mourning. For example, David ended his period of mourning for his and Bathsheba's son by washing, using lotions and getting changed (2 Samuel 12:20).

Perhaps the writer of Ruth's story has both ideas in mind in verse 3. Ruth may have been in mourning for her husband up to this point. Naomi is encouraging her to return to normality and take up the search for a new husband. Also, the meeting on the threshing-floor was to be a special event; after all, Naomi expects it to result in a new home for Ruth. So she wants Ruth to follow some of the same routine as a bride would before her wedding.

The other interesting aspect of verse 3 is that it introduces the element of secrecy which marks the events of this chapter. Ruth is to hide from Boaz until he has enjoyed his evening meal. Presumably this implies that Boaz will be fully content as he settles down to rest. Then Ruth is to uncover his feet and also lie down. However we interpret this, it is a risky move. It may mean that Ruth is to uncover just his feet, or possibly the whole of his body from the waist down. It may mean that Ruth and Boaz are to lie down together as man and wife, or simply that Ruth is to lie close by, indicating she is available for marriage. Because of Boaz's reaction to Ruth's actions (verse 10), it is normally assumed that he, at least, understands her to be symbolically requesting marriage. Naomi does not tell Ruth to voice such a request; perhaps this would put Ruth's modesty and integrity in doubt. But Naomi's instructions are full of provocative overtones, and Ruth's compliance with them surely expresses sexual attraction and tension.

Again Ruth faces a critical choice, just as on the road to Judah (chapter 1). How should she respond to Naomi's scheme? Ruth boldly commits herself to follow Naomi's plan despite all the risks involved (verse 5).

Questions

1. Are you the sort of person who 'makes things happen'?

Why? Why not? How do you feel when your plans (or someone else's) succeed?

2. Naomi's plan was really the answer to her own prayers. How might God want us to act to answer our own prayers in our church life at the moment?

3. We can get lots of advice about lots of things in today's world: pensions, mortgages, careers, relationships, politics, morality, childcare, health … Whose advice do you value? How do you decide when to follow advice? Are you as good at following advice as you are at giving it?

3

GOD WORKS ALL THINGS FOR GOOD

Ruth 3:6 – 4:22

What do you really make of Romans 8:28: 'And we know that in all things God works for the good of those who love him, who have been called according to his purpose'? Do you really feel that God is working for your good at the moment? We may be aware that God is 'good' (see, for example, Psalms 100:5; 145:9), and that his people are the recipients of his goodness (see, for example, Psalm 73:1). But perhaps our situation may best be described as bitter misery and affliction (compare Ruth 1:20–21). How can God be working for my good when the boundary lines have not fallen for me in pleasant places (contrast Psalm 16:6)? The challenge of verses like Romans 8:28 is to focus on God's eternal good purposes and to let our immediate circumstances fade and blur. Romans 8 contrasts our present circumstances with 'the glory that will be revealed in us' (verse 18). But Paul is not just looking to the future. In Romans 8 he suggests that we can experience the love and gracious goodness of God even in trouble, hardship, persecution, famine, nakedness, danger or sword (verses 35–36). As he explains, 'God is for us' (verse 31). That truth can be our present experience as well as our future hope.

In Ruth 3 – 4 the immediate physical needs of Ruth and Naomi begin to fade and blur. Coming into sharp focus is the realization that 'God is for' these two women. A series of astounding events builds up to the climax, 'Praise be to the LORD' (4:14). This is the climax of Ruth's story, for it interprets all that has happened. The story is not just about coincidences and kind people like Boaz. It is about God working for the good of his people. It affirms that God's goodness does not end when problems begin. It reminds us that God works within history and within our circumstances. In his goodness God intervenes, and in so doing he draws his committed people to himself. The book of Ruth shows us that when God's people co-operate with his plans, they learn about him and his ways. Perhaps Ruth would be first in line to echo the words of the psalmist, 'You are good and what you do is good … It was good for me to be afflicted so that I might learn your decrees' (Psalm 119:68, 71).

Ruth 3:6–15

Reputations risked

Ruth speaks with Boaz on the threshing-floor during the night. She leaves secretly in the morning.

Is there anything worth risking your reputation for? Ruth obviously thought Boaz was well worth the risk! This meeting on the threshing-floor could undermine the good reputation that Ruth had earned for herself since her arrival in Bethlehem. To meet a man in secrecy in the night and then lie down with him is not acceptable behaviour. It is provocative and shows no respect for social constraints. In short, it is disgraceful behaviour, to be ashamed of. Each character (and reader of the story) nervously anticipates Boaz's response.

These verses are full of ambiguity, mystery and intrigue. It seems as if the writer is at pains to keep the details of this encounter to a minimum, so that its central elements remain plain.

Ruth obeys instructions

Ruth follows up her words (verse 5) with action (verse 6). There is no mention of delay. She simply gets on with doing everything Naomi has suggested. Now we see why Naomi advised Ruth to wait until Boaz was physically refreshed (verse 3). Having had a meal, Boaz is 'in good spirits' (or 'his heart was good'; verse 7). Naomi certainly didn't want a tired and grumpy man meeting Ruth in these unacceptable circumstances. Ruth herself is sensitive to the precarious nature of her actions. She wisely approaches 'quietly', uncovers Boaz's feet and lies down. Naomi had not specified where Ruth should lie down. In fact, Ruth chose to lie down by Boaz's feet (verse 8). The feet were often associated both with humility (particularly in front of someone who is superior in some way) and with making a request, so Ruth's choice of position is appropriate and modest. The purpose of uncovering Boaz's feet is not clear. As we saw in the last study, perhaps this was part of the ritual associated with asking for marriage (especially if 'feet' are a polite way of referring to the lower part of the body). Maybe the writer is simply giving a reason for Boaz's sudden awakening – he had cold feet!

Verse 9 marks a break with the instructions Naomi gave. Ruth has to use her own initiative as she responds to Boaz's question about her identity. His question contrasts with his earlier one, 'Whose young woman is that?' (2:5). Now he is more direct. Ruth gives her name and her status. She is still restrained, but she is now bold enough to say that she is Boaz's servant without the qualification she felt obliged to add in 2:13. But she discards all restraint when she says, 'Spread the corner of your garment over me since you are a kinsman-redeemer.'

Her request has four implications:

▶ First, it implies that Ruth recognizes her own need for protection (the word for 'corner' is the same as the word for 'wing' used in 2:12). In other words, Ruth asks Boaz to be the answer to his own prayer for her safety.

▶ Secondly, it was customary for a widow's relative to claim his right to marry her by covering her with a garment. If Ruth has this in mind (as Boaz's response suggests she did), then she is asking Boaz for his hand in marriage.

▶ Thirdly, if we compare Ruth's words with Ezekiel 16:8, it appears that Ruth is suggesting to Boaz that she is ready to assume sexual relations with him by becoming his bride.

▶ Fourthly, Ruth makes her request because Boaz is her 'kinsman-redeemer'. What she does is not improper or immoral, but justified. She shows respect for the law about kinsman-redeemers, but in fact asks Boaz to go beyond the requirements of the law (to redeem land) by redeeming Ruth herself (by meeting her need for a husband).

Ruth's words are few, but their significance is great. She says nothing else to Boaz, but humbly submits to his instructions.

Boaz responds favourably

The response Ruth receives is immediately and obviously favourable (verse 10). Another blessing is given and again Ruth's kindness is praised. Twice Boaz calls her 'my daughter', which conveys a close relationship and a desire to protect and provide for her. It also suggests that Ruth is younger than Boaz. This ties in with the reason for Boaz's praise for Ruth. She has been kind to Boaz by placing her trust in him and her affections on him and not on younger men. There is something impressive about this romance; it is not 'heady', but well considered.

The theme of Ruth's noble character is picked up in verse 11. Her actions have risked her reputation, but Boaz reassures her that nothing is lost. The Hebrew word translated 'noble character' is used to describe Boaz in 2:1 ('of standing'). The word means 'strength (of character)', so the writer is saying that Boaz's strength of character is matched by Ruth's own. In other words, these two truly deserve each other. Despite the age gap, this is an ideal match.

But verses 11–12 interrupt the developing story. Ruth, who arrived with Naomi empty-handed, discovers that she has one helper too many. It is a mark of Boaz's respect for the law that he recognizes the rights of her closer relative. At the same time he does not use this as an excuse: his desire to act as redeemer is clear from the oath, 'If he is not willing, as surely as the LORD lives, I will do it' (verse 13). Also, he is willing to risk his reputation for Ruth. It is he who encourages Ruth to stay for the night. In fact, more significantly, she is to lie down (verse 13). We might be eager to find out more about the night's events, but the writer has decided to keep them a mystery. There is nothing to suggest that Ruth and Boaz did anything other than sleep. But she leaves secretly and is sworn to secrecy (verse 14). This serves to protect Ruth and Boaz from charges of improper behaviour, and also safeguards Boaz's plan when he speaks with the nearer relative (chapter 4).

The tense scene ends with a practical gift (verse 15). To his positive response and promise Boaz adds a large gift of barley. In so doing he meets Ruth's short-term needs as well as the long-term ones. It is possible that this gift of barley was meant as payment for Ruth as the bride price or as a marriage gift. More simply, it shows us that Naomi's needs have not been forgotten (for the story began with her and is to end with her). The further act of kindness which concludes this scene helps the reader to anticipate Ruth's blessed future, which will end her days of emptiness. This unconventional event has not destroyed reputations but has enhanced them. Boaz now goes back to town to make the necessary arrangements.

Meanwhile, Ruth reports back to Naomi. Her mother-in-law's question is literally, 'Who are you, my daughter?' (verse 16). This is difficult to understand, because the first part of the question appears to be answered in the second. It could be translated, 'What are you feeling like?', or even 'Who are you feeling like?', so maybe Naomi is really asking Ruth whether she is feeling like Boaz's wife yet! Again, this debrief seems to resound with excitement. Ruth pours out the events in detail to Naomi (verses 16–17). It is important to note that Boaz's love for Ruth extends also to Naomi. The measures of barley provided by Boaz for Naomi mean that Naomi's plan, though quite selfless, is beginning to result in her blessing too.

Naomi's advice to Ruth to wait (verse 18) is her last recorded utterance. No more words of Ruth are recorded either. The women have played their part, and Boaz takes charge from here on. Naomi knows that both she and Ruth can sit tight. She is confident that their 'kinsman-redeemer' will settle everything straight away.

Questions

1. A number of aspects of the relationship between Ruth and Boaz might trouble us: Ruth is about to marry a man who is significantly older than she is; *she* has asked for *his* hand in marriage; she has been married before; they are from different cultural backgrounds. What aspects of the marriages of our own friends and family do we find difficult to accept? Why?

2. Imagine you are a minister or leader in a local church. Ruth and Boaz come to you for their pre-marriage counselling course. What issues do you discuss with them?

3. In what circumstances, if any, do you think it is acceptable to ignore normal social and moral constraints?

Ruth 4:1–6

Boaz takes charge

───────────────

Boaz negotiates with Naomi's nearer relative at the town gates. The nearer relative gives up his right to redeem Naomi's land.

'Knowing what you want is only half the task. Getting what you want is what really matters.' How often have you heard a comment like this? Many business people earn their fortune by adopting this ruthless, self-centred approach. Boaz's wish is clear. He wants to act as redeemer for Ruth (3:13), but how is he to achieve this? In these six verses Boaz's plan unfolds. He gets what he wants, and, although his plan is clever and determined, he is neither ruthless nor selfish. In fact, he stands in contrast to the nearer relative, who is concerned with his own material well-being. Boaz is concerned with Ruth's well-being, and is presumably driven by his love for her.

The court sits

At the end of chapter 3 Ruth is told to wait to see what happens. Just as Naomi anticipated, Boaz gets on with sorting things out. He goes to the town gates because that was the most likely place where he would meet his relative. Everyone congregated there, especially if there were matters to discuss or sort out. A modern-day equivalent would be a pub, coffee house or clubhouse. But these examples do not closely compare with the formal legal procedures that took place at the town gates. The respected elders and leaders of a town met here to hear legal cases and pronounce judgments. So once his relative arrives, Boaz calls a court to session. He selects 'ten of the elders of the town' (verse 2). This number may just be a loose figure (compare the phrase 'after they had lived there about ten years', 1:4), but it does suggest that a sizeable small group assembled. Note that it is Boaz who gives the orders. He is really in charge of the discussion and controls the proceedings.

In our English translation, 'my friend' (verse 1) suggests a relaxed atmosphere. While there is nothing in the text which denies this possibility, the phrase could equally be translated 'So-and-so' – much less friendly. Both translations give us the impression that this man and Boaz did not enjoy a close relationship. Boaz never uses the other's name, and the relative remains anonymous. It seems that the writer is trying to ensure that this new character does not become too important in the story.

The issue of the land

Boaz's first words to his relative concern a piece of land belonging to Naomi (verse 3). This is a surprise, because we thought Naomi was destitute, and certainly Ruth's gleaning work added to this impression. It is possible that when Naomi left Bethlehem with Elimelech, they left behind a piece of land which others had since cultivated. (This is the situation which the Shunammite woman faced after living in Philistine territory; see 2 Kings 8:1–6.) Perhaps Naomi could claim this land back after it had yielded its harvest, even though her poverty meant she needed to sell it. Whatever the precise circumstances, it is clear that

▶ Boaz knows about the piece of land;
▶ he is aware of Naomi's legal position;
▶ he knows that she wants to sell the land;
▶ he is comfortable about settling this matter on her behalf.

All this suggests that Boaz is already working for the well-being of Naomi and Ruth. He has already assumed responsibility for at least some of their legal affairs. We can only presume that the nearer relative was not aware of this land and his rights to it. Boaz acts honourably. He pays attention to legal procedures and makes the situation known before witnesses (verse 4). It is not surprising that the initial response of the unnamed relative is, 'I will redeem it.' The land could be purchased at a cheap price and, he thought, there were no relatives who could reclaim it in the future.

The issue of Ruth

All seems well for the unnamed relative until Ruth is mentioned (verse 5). Suddenly the rights of the kinsman don't seem so attractive. Boaz claims that the name of Elimelech should be maintained alongside his property. Ruth is the means of providing Elimelech with an heir. Again Boaz uses the description 'the Moabitess', underlining Ruth's foreign identity. It is unclear whether Boaz is suggesting that his relative will acquire Ruth or that he himself will take Ruth as a wife (some texts have 'you acquire', others 'I acquire'). The point is that in either case Ruth would probably produce an heir who would be entitled to claim back the land. The kinsman is being asked to make an investment that won't pay off. For the sake of his own financial security he tells Boaz, 'You redeem it yourself. I cannot do it' (verse 6). Boaz is willing, eager and able to redeem Naomi's land and her family. As a man motivated by love and kindness, he will act as redeemer despite the circumstances. His concern for Ruth and Naomi supersedes his self-interest.

Questions

1. It seems that taking on the duties of kinsman-redeemer was to some extent voluntary. The responsibility could be passed on to someone else. What family responsibilities do we consider to be compulsory or voluntary?

What motivates us in this area?

2. How much importance do we attach to acting honourably when something is important to us? How can Boaz's example be followed in church life?

3. In what situations today do people call witnesses? How seriously should we take the responsibilities of being a 'witness'?

The town gate

This is the term used for a spacious area just by the gate in the town wall. It was a place of trade (Genesis 23:10–11; 2 Kings 7:1, 18) as well as a meeting-place where legal assemblies were held (Genesis 34:19–20; Deuteronomy 22:13–19). Punishment could be carried out at the gate (Deuteronomy 21:18–21). Field workers met at the gate as they went out to labour on the farmland. Travellers to other towns and cities would have to leave through the town gates. So the town-gate area was fundamental to the operations of town life. It is little wonder that it was here that prophets would often address the people (Jeremiah 17:19–20). The town gate was a public area with public access. By taking such an area as its setting, Ruth 4 provides a contrast with the secret and private setting of chapter 3.

Levirate marriage

This is a custom known from the regulations in Deuteronomy 25:5–10. The word 'levirate' is based on the Latin word *levir*, which means 'brother-in-law', but could possibly also be used in the sense of 'relative'.

The law regarding levirate marriage required the brother of a man who had died to marry the widow. This was intended in order to provide an heir to maintain the family line. Deuteronomy 25 specifies that the law applied to brothers who were living together. An example of this levirate marriage is Onan's marriage to Tamar in Genesis 38, though in this case the union did not achieve its stated objectives.

It is possible that Ruth's request and Boaz's negotiations were based on the principle of levirate marriage – but no brother who lived with Mahlon exists, so Ruth's story is about someone going beyond the expectations of the law. Boaz is not obliged to marry Ruth: his actions stem from his kindness to Ruth, which has repeatedly exceeded expectation. The lifestyle and attitudes commended to us in this story are revolutionary. They demand much more than merely living according to legal and social regulations.

Ruth 4:7–12

Wedding bells

Boaz formally receives the rights of kinsman-redeemer. Everyone wishes Boaz and Ruth blessings in their marriage.

Nothing stirs us up like the prospect of a fairytale wedding. Do you remember the excitement about the wedding of the Prince of Wales to Lady Diana  Spencer? A young kindergarten teacher was to marry the most eligible bachelor in the country. Tied up with that was the hope that this young woman would bear an heir to the throne. What's more, we were led to believe that the Queen Mother had a lot to do with the blossoming of the romance. There are many parallels with the Ruth and Boaz story. Ruth was young and emerged from obscurity. Naomi, a relative of Boaz, is involved in orchestrating the romance. Boaz is well known, respected and wealthy but had no heir. We know from the final verses of chapter 4 that from this marriage a royal line stemmed. It is little wonder that the people joined with the elders of the town to give their blessing to this marriage (4:11). The story is reaching its climax and we are not disappointed by its outcome.

Boaz becomes kinsman-redeemer

Verses 7–8 emphasize that Boaz receives the legal right to redeem the land. No-one could contest Boaz's rights, because

▶ witnesses are present to confirm the transaction (verses 4, 9);

▶ the transaction follows accepted procedures for redeeming and transferring property (verse 7);

▶ the nearer relative shows his consent and sincerity by the symbolic act of removing his sandal (verse 8).

The benefits of this transferral of rights are summarized in Boaz's acceptance speech in verses 9–10, which he begins and ends with the words, 'Today you are witnesses.' Boaz fulfils the confidence Naomi has in him: 'the man will not rest until the matter is settled today' (3:18). He acts swiftly but precisely to settle the matter once and for all. By mentioning the names of Elimelech, Kilion and Mahlon, Boaz shows he is taking on responsibility for the complete family line, not just Ruth's branch through Mahlon. His purpose in taking Ruth as his wife is to maintain the family name with the property. Maintaining the family name and providing for the widow is what lay behind the laws regarding levirate marriage and kinsman-redeemers. Boaz, motivated by lovingkindness, chooses to take upon himself responsibilities that he is not obliged to exercise. In so doing he wins Ruth as his wife. His purpose achieved, he takes no further verbal part in this story.

Congratulations and God bless you!

There is obvious pleasure at this outcome. The elders, who are the legal witnesses, and everyone else unite to bless Ruth and Boaz. They desire the couple's happiness and well-being. The detailed and specific blessing has three parts:

▶ *May Ruth be like Rachel and Leah.* This focuses on Ruth. Rachel and Leah were the mothers of the house of Israel. The blessing includes the wish that Ruth will, like them, produce a great line of descendants. It may also include the desire that Ruth may be dearly loved like Rachel and very fertile like Leah (see Genesis 29).

▶ *May Boaz be respected and famous.* This focuses on Boaz. The exact meaning of this second part is difficult. The general request is that Boaz will enjoy honour among his own people. It may also intend to wish him power and prosperity. These will be achieved through his wife and his children. So this central part of the blessing links its three parts together.

▶ *May your family be like Perez' family.* This focuses on the couple's children. The blessing expresses the wish that Boaz's family will become important. Perez is generally considered to be the father of the most important family line within Judah. Both this and the first part of the blessing refer to the Lord as the one who gives children. This suggests that with the Lord's help Ruth will bear more than just one child. The reference to the Lord's help is significant for at least two reasons. First, Ruth's previous marriage had not produced children. Secondly, the Lord's intervention legitimizes the contribution of Ruth (the Moabitess) to the line of David. Note that Tamar too is mentioned; she, like Ruth, was a foreigner.

So wedding bells are in the air and everyone is pleased about it. Everyone wishes Ruth and Boaz blessing from the Lord.

Questions

1. Think about what you want to get out of your business transactions, your marriage or your relationships. Why can symbols be important to contracts we make?
2. How do we pray for engaged couples or newlyweds in our churches? How can we be more specific and forward-looking when we pray for them?
3. Why do people get married? Think about different cultures and the way arranged marriages operate. How important are children to marriage today?

Removing sandals

The explanation of the custom of removing a sandal (verse 7) rather intrudes into the narrative: it gives the impression that the author is writing some time after the event, and that the procedure needs to be explained because it would make no sense to those for whom the story was written.

Although there are many references to the removal of shoes in the Old Testament, each reference seems to symbolize something different. For example, it could show personal unworthiness (Exodus 3:5; Joshua 5:15) or mourning (Ezekiel 24:17, 23). There is also an association with possessing land (Psalm 60:8). From Deuteronomy 25:5–10 we know that the removal of a sandal conferred shame on someone unwilling to take on levirate marriage responsibilities. In Ruth 4 the mention of the removal of the sandal recalls this idea and therefore casts at least some degree of disgrace on the unwilling nearer relative. More explicitly, the procedure is mentioned because it gives Boaz legal rights as the sole kinsman-redeemer. It is worth noting that when Jeremiah buys a field, different procedures are in place to legitimize the purchase (Jeremiah 32:10–15). This change of procedure may account for the need to explain the action in Ruth 4:7.

Ruth 4:13–22

A son is born

Ruth's son and Naomi's grandson Obed is born. Naomi's friends give her a blessing and a promise. Obed becomes the grandfather of King David.

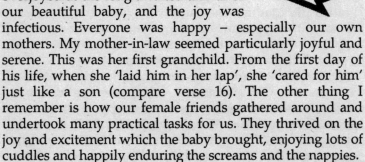

I remember the birth of my first son very well. My husband and I were overjoyed at the long-awaited arrival of our beautiful baby, and the joy was infectious. Everyone was happy – especially our own mothers. My mother-in-law seemed particularly joyful and serene. This was her first grandchild. From the first day of his life, when she 'laid him in her lap', she 'cared for him' just like a son (compare verse 16). The other thing I remember is how our female friends gathered around and undertook many practical tasks for us. They thrived on the joy and excitement which the baby brought, enjoying lots of cuddles and happily enduring the screams and the nappies.

These memories are similar to the scene in these verses.

The men, who dominated the chapter to this point, disappear. Naomi embraces her first grandchild, and her friends celebrate and say wonderful things about all the joy this child will bring. Just as chapter 1 gives the female perspective on Naomi's status as a desolate widow, chapter 4 ends with the same perspective on her status as a joyful grandparent.

Naomi has a son again!

These verses are stunning because Ruth and Boaz take back stage while Naomi receives all the congratulations. Many new mums would be just a little put out if their mothers-in-law achieved this! Verse 13 skips over the wedding events and rushes to tell us that Ruth gives birth to a son. The little phrase 'the LORD enabled her to conceive' reminds us that children are a gift from the Lord (Psalm 127:3). Our attention is also drawn to the fact that earlier prayers for Ruth are now being answered (Ruth 1:8–9; 4:11). This means that God's blessing rests upon this marriage. The impression is that they didn't have to wait very long for this confirmation.

The birth of the baby boy is greeted with words of praise from Naomi's female friends (verse 14). This contrasts with the earlier scene when the women had heard only bitter news that apparently reduced them to silence (1:19–21). Their rejoicing begins at the right place. They thank God for his provision for Naomi. They refer to the newborn baby as Naomi's kinsman-redeemer; someone who will preserve her family name and protect her. Such a role is usually associated with a son, not a grandson. The story has developed in a way that allows Ruth's son to provide the security and hope of which Naomi was bereft at its start. The women move from praise to prayer: 'May he become famous throughout Israel!' This is a bold request that goes beyond the expectations of the prayer for Boaz (verse 11). What a contrast! The elders of the town (and others) had faith to pray that Boaz would be well known in Bethlehem, but these unnamed women prayed that this young child, born of a foreign mother, would be famous in the whole of Israel. What a prayer of faith! We might even argue that this is a prophetic prayer. It is clearly inspired by the women's joy for Naomi and their respect for Ruth and her son.

So with confidence they move from prayer to promise (verse 15). They believe that this child will give Naomi a new lease of life that will last to old age. In other words they affirm that Naomi now has a future and a hope centred upon all that this child represents. This new life will fill the void left by her widowhood and bereavement. It is a life which originates with the Lord and with Ruth who 'has given him birth' (verse 15). The women make the astonishing claim that Ruth is better to Naomi 'than seven sons'. Having numerous sons was considered a sign of great blessing (Psalm 127:4-5), so it is remarkable to say that Ruth, a single daughter-in-law, was of greater worth than these. This again suggests that the story is written from a female point of view, but it also comes in the context of Ruth's love for Naomi. This has been demonstrated throughout the story, and it seems appropriate that Ruth is commended for her love for Naomi as it concludes.

Verses 16–17 present one final image. Naomi cares for Ruth's son, and together the women agree on the name 'Obed' which means 'servant'. Verse 16 suggests that an intimate and caring relationship is formed between Naomi and Obed. This provided Naomi with status and a role again. Her arms are no longer empty, but full. She is restored through Obed, who serves to bring the Lord's blessing to her.

Boaz has a royal descendant

Verses 18–22 give a long-term view of the significance of Naomi's story. They list ten generations of Boaz's family line, beginning with Perez and ending with King David. These verses tell us about God's developing purposes. The story of Ruth shows how God works with his people, through their co-operation and prayers, to bring blessing. The lovingkindness his people have shown to each other mirrors the Lord's own kindness to his people. Individuals find that their situation is turned round completely. In desperation they discover deliverance, and through deliverance they find their place in God's good purposes.

Eventually the whole nation of Israel is blessed as a result of this family. From this family the great king David emerges. Through this family line the hope is kindled for a redeemer who, in keeping with God's purpose, will bring hope and a future not just to a single family but to the whole world. To the whole world, centuries later, comes the good news of great joy which the angel brings: 'In the town of David a Saviour has been born to you; he is Christ the Lord' (Luke 2:11).

The story of Ruth illustrates what salvation really means. The poor and needy turn to the Lord and are saved (Isaiah 45:22).

Questions

1. From your own experience, recall times when the Lord has turned your life around. Don't forget to use your memories to praise God.
2. Think of the people in your church who do the ordinary, mundane tasks. How does God fulfil his purposes through them? Try to encourage them this week.
3. Try to put yourself in the position of a childless couple who want children, or a bereaved person. What can you do to ease their pain and sorrow?

The Lord as redeemer

In the book of Ruth, Boaz is described as Ruth's kinsman-redeemer. But Ruth's story (as we have seen) urges us to think of her God as her ultimate redeemer. Boaz co-operates with God's plans and the result is redemption for Ruth and her family. Eventually the family line, established through Ruth and Boaz, gives rise to Jesus, the redeemer of the world. Ruth herself is mentioned in the genealogy of Jesus in Matthew 1:5. Matthew says Jesus will be called 'Immanuel', 'God with us' (1:23). Through the Lord Jesus Christ we know God's presence with us. For God 'has rescued us from the dominion of darkness and brought us into the kingdom of the Son he loves, in whom we have redemption, the forgiveness of sins' (Colossians 1:13–14). It was by God's presence with Ruth, mediated by her kinsman-redeemer, that her 'kingdom of darkness' was turned into an experience of joy, love and hope. Ruth took refuge in the God of Israel, and in so doing she took her place in God's redemptive purposes. We too are invited to participate in God's work by finding our refuge in him through 'Immanuel', our Lord Jesus Christ.

THE BOOK OF ESTHER

Why read the book of Esther?

The story of Esther is about a young Jewish woman and her uncle, who manage to secure the future of the Jewish people living under the Persian empire. Their success explains the origins of a Jewish festival, Purim, which has celebrated their victory ever since.

On the surface, God is absent from this great event of deliverance. In fact, God is not mentioned in the book at all! But a careful reading of the story shows us that far from being absent, God is hidden in the story. If we take notice of the clues, we realize that God is the central character. At strategic moments, God's controlling presence and purpose are assumed. It is as if his involvement is so obvious that it need not be mentioned. In the light of this perspective, the details of the story find their meaning. Because the Lord is present with his people, Esther's uncle Mordecai is certain that the Jews will be delivered (Esther 4:14). Because God cares for his people, fasting has a purpose (4:3, 16). God's involvement with his people explains why Haman's advisors hold the Jewish people in awe (6:13). We can take it that these assumptions are part of the mindset of the original readers of the story. The writer does not need to tell them what they already know. Instead, the writer confirms that these assumptions are right, because they are the foundation of all human experience – whether we choose to recognize it or not.

Despite this, the book of Esther has not always been recognized as confirming and commending faith in God. Even the great Reformer Martin Luther doubted whether it should be included in the Old Testament. In contrast, the early Jewish scholars who translated the Old Testament from Hebrew into Greek added six new sections to the story, which specifically celebrate God's work. While these translators show a certain lack of appreciation for the writer's own perspective on the story, they do at least indicate that very early on God was recognized as the hidden and central character in the story. They did not want to keep God hidden between the lines. They wanted to make explicit what the author implied.

Indeed, this book doesn't make sense without God. It confirms that God's purpose to bring relief and salvation to his people will not be thwarted by Haman or anyone else. This is why the book of Esther has many parallels to the exodus story. Circumstances have changed, but God has not. Just as he heard the cry of his oppressed people in Egypt (Exodus 6:5), now he hears the wailing of his people facing the terror of Haman (Esther 4:1–3). Once his people faced the terror of Egypt; now some of his people are experiencing a vindictive Persian official. But God's promises are unchanged. His people will always experience deliverance and salvation because he remembers his covenant (Exodus 6:5). So God's actions in saving and delivering his people are worth remembering and celebrating. By so doing we recognize that God is active and pre-eminent in human affairs.

Like the story of Ruth, Esther's story is full of practical and spiritual help. Both stories encourage us to delve beneath the surface of our circumstances to discover God's protecting wings of refuge (Ruth 2:12). This discovery brings relief, joy and celebration (Esther 9:22) as it transforms our restricted view of God into limitless wonder.

A note on authorship, setting and dating

The author of the book of Esther is not known, though it seems certain that he or she was a Jew writing between 460 and 330 BC. The story is set in the reign of King Xerxes (486–465 BC), and therefore comes in the sixty-year gap presumed between the events of chapters 6 and 7 of the book of Ezra. During this time some of the exiled Jews returned to

Jerusalem, but others remained in Mesopotamia under Persian rule. The Jews who remained were aware that their positon was rather tenuous. In the person of Haman their fears were realized, for he threatened to destroy the Jewish people once again. In the light of the terror Haman represented to God's people, it is remarkable that the role of a Jewish woman is so important. Esther co-operates with Mordecai and plays a crucial part in saving God's people. It is a role she alone can undertake. Esther is not restricted by her gender, despite the lowly status of women in her culture. This author appreciates that everyone has the opportunity to co-operate with God's purposes.

GOD WORKS IN MYSTERIOUS WAYS

Esther 1 – 2

Esther 1:1–22

Feasting turns to fury

King Xerxes' banquet is ruined by Queen Vashti's refusal to entertain his guests. Vashti loses her royal status.

Feasting is an important theme throughout the story of Esther. In chapter 1, a series of banquets celebrates the power and splendour of the Persian king.  This helps us to appreciate something of the vulnerability of the Jewish people who find themselves living within this prosperous empire. But this first chapter also shows a number of alarming aspects of the leadership in the city of Susa. Xerxes, as king, is the key player, but he is supported by a range of named and unnamed officials who actually seem to control his activities.

As we start to look at the story, it is helpful to realize that the plot eventually turns full circle. The book of Esther concludes with another feast, the feast of Purim (chapter 9), and with another powerful and great leader, Mordecai the Jew. In contrast to the banquets in chapter 1, the Purim feast celebrates not human power but the supernatural deliverance of the Jews from their powerful enemies. God's people can always be courageous, for God is able to turn things around completely.

The good life

Verses 1–9 tell us that the third year of the reign of king Xerxes was marked by celebratory banquets. The section is constructed around the repeated words 'he/the king/ Queen Vashti gave a banquet' in verses 3, 5 and 9. The first two occurrences of this phrase are followed by elaborate descriptions of the banquets. This contrasts with the lack of detail of the third banquet, the one hosted by the queen. It is the excesses of the Persian king which are emphasized. This even influences the way his authority is described in verse 1. His rule extends 'over 127 provinces stretching from India to Cush'. Actually there were only thirty-one provinces. The writer is possibly counting the sub-divisions within provinces, using the larger number because it conveys more clearly the vastness of the Persian empire, and draws attention to its extensive administrative system.

The first banquet has two notable features:

▶ it is attended by a vast array of the king's leaders and officials (verse 3), and

▶ its length is excessive ('a full 180 days', verse 4).

The writer is set on making the banquet seem ridiculous. 'What would a six-month banquet be like? How could so many people be entertained successfully for so long?' But even more incredible details follow about the second feast. While much less excessive in length ('lasting seven days', verse 5), this royal banquet is for everyone who is allowed into the royal area of Susa (called the 'citadel'). It is held in the king's open-air garden, which is decorated to show off his splendour and extravagance. It's as if the king is hosting an exhibition to celebrate his own achievements. Verses 6–7 suggests that we should be overwhelmed by what is being described. We are encouraged to imagine the garden with its white and blue hangings, with its marble and mother-of-pearl pavement. There is nothing modest about the scene. No expense is spared, and the drink flowed freely (verses 7–8). Surely a king who shows no restraint in his own luxurious lifestyle couldn't expect others to show restraint. In fact, liberality marks his character. Xerxes is really telling everyone to do as they please.

Verse 9 is remarkable in contrast. The queen's banquet was apparently nothing special. Certainly it doesn't warrant detailed and lavish description. Verse 9 shows us a gulf between the king and his queen. As the story continues, that gulf becomes unbridgeable.

It is worth noting that these banquets serve no specific purpose. No one event seems to prompt these celebrations. The only clue we get is in verse 4, which tells us that the king spent the duration of the second feast showing off. He wants his wealth, splendour and glory to be recognized by everyone. It is to be expected, then, that all who threaten the image he wants to propagate would place themselves outside his favour. We have here a leader totally consumed by egotism. This fact is so vital to the story that the writer emphasizes it at every opportunity in this opening section.

Vashti is made an example

The idyllic scene is abruptly disrupted by the events recorded in verses 10–22. This happens because Xerxes still wants to show off more of his good life to those around him. These verses tell how Vashti is punished because she refuses to be party to his boasting. There is a great deal of irony:

▶ Vashti decides that she won't parade herself before the people and nobles, but she is accused of disrespect (verse 18) rather than commended for protecting the king from his own misjudgment.

▶ The king's 'wise' advisors act without reference to the law or common sense. They presume that Vashti's 'disobedience' will be followed by every other wife (verse 18).

▶ The king is portrayed as rather useless. He doesn't confront his wife himself. His ego is hurt and all he is capable of is fury (verse 12).

The other interesting feature of these verses is that Vashti takes no direct part in the story. She is the cause of the events recorded rather than a participator in them. She does not come privately to the king to explain her actions. Just as we expect on the evidence of verse 9, the worlds of the king and the queen remain separate. The result is that Vashti's integrity is not tainted by the king's lack of it. She retains her dignity.

Verses 10–12 suggest that Vashti's refusal is wise. The king and his companions have had a lot to drink. The gathering could easily develop into something like a drunken orgy. When the Bible describes someone as 'high in spirits' because of wine (verse 10), the implication is that they lack sound judgment. (A useful parallel is 1 Samuel 25:36–37, where Abigail waited until morning to speak with Nabal, because he was drunk after holding 'a banquet like that of a king'.) A team of eunuchs is sent to collect Vashti (verses 10–11). Perhaps Xerxes considers her the crowning glory of his material possessions. Certainly her non-compliance with his plans is an incredible snub to the pomp arranged for her appearance before the people and nobles. Xerxes wants her to appear (possibly naked) in front of other people, and it is this that she refuses to do. She did not refuse to appear before her husband alone so that he could enjoy her beauty.

Verses 13–22 describe the decision to dispose of Vashti. Another list of names appears (verse 13) and one of these men, Memucan, takes a leading role in encouraging Xerxes to make a hasty royal decree. The advice Memucan gives is pragmatic rather than based on any law (which is supposed to be his area of expertise). It seems that Memucan is personally affronted by Vashti (verse 16) – after all, as a noble, he too had been denied the opportunity to admire Vashti's beauty. His main concern seems to be to get even with Vashti for refusing to perform for him and his friends. In the light of this, his words about submission and respect for husbands seem more of an excuse than a reason for the punishment Vashti receives.

Verse 22 rounds off the narrative with more irony. Once again, with typical Persian efficiency and attention to detail, the decree is dispatched to each province. We are reminded of the opening verse of the chapter. Xerxes may be morally weak. He may have lost his beautiful queen as a result of too much drink and too much pride. But he is powerful. The Persian Empire is a dangerous environment and the Persian palace is a volatile place. The political and moral context of the story is clear. The stage is set. It is this stage that Esther will grace with her presence.

Questions

1. What dangers do we face when we feel personally affronted or falsely accused? Whose advice do we usually prefer to follow?
2. In what circumstances are we sometimes tempted to show off, and why? What are the consequences of this to individuals and to churches?
3. What moral dangers do world leaders and their advisors face today? How do their responses to such dangers influence the way we view them?

Beyond understanding

How many times have you been consoled by the thought that God's work is mysterious and far beyond our understanding?

On one level, to be told that something is a mystery doesn't help very much at all. Think of young children coming to terms with the world and its complexities. They are always asking, 'Why?' 'How?' 'Where?' and 'When?' I am reminded of this every day. My four-year-old son asks questions at a phenomenal rate – and woe betide me if I can't give a sensible answer. 'Mummy, how does electricity make lights work? Why are plugs dangerous? How many people are there in the whole world? How much do I love you today? If God is baby Jesus, how did he put that big tree over there? How can God have the whole world in his hands if his arms are straight and the world is round?'

We have a natural desire to understand and unravel the mysteries we meet. But when it comes to matters of faith and belief, our explanations will always fail, at least to some extent. This doesn't mean that we should stop trying to express our faith. Rather, we need to confess the limitations of our human understanding. To admit that God's ways are mysterious is itself a step of faith. Isaiah records God's own claim: 'As the heavens are higher than the earth, so are my ways higher than your ways' (Isaiah 55:9). Job confesses, 'God is greater than man' (Job 33:12), and cries, 'How great is God – beyond our understanding!' (Job 36:26). It is a theme taken up in both Ephesians and Colossians, which refer to 'the mystery of [God's] will' (Ephesians 1:9; compare Colossians 1:25 – 2:3). Recognizing the limits of our human understanding is a step of faith that William Cowper commends to us in his hymn written at the end of the eighteenth century:

> God moves in a mysterious way,
>   His wonders to perform;
> He plants his footstep in the sea,
>   And rides upon the storm.
>
> Deep in unfathomable mines
>   Of never-failing skill,
> He treasures up his bright designs,
>   And works his sovereign will.
>
> Ye fearful saints, fresh courage take;
>   The clouds ye so much dread
> Are big with mercy, and shall break
>   In blessings on your head.

This hymn is very appropriate to our study of Esther, particularly chapters 1 – 2. The events recorded here are culturally remote and difficult for us to appreciate fully. We don't know quite what to make of Vashti or, for that matter, Esther. There are parallels between these two women, yet the contrast in their fortunes is pronounced. But behind the puzzling opening scene the message is plain. God is at work, mysterious and hidden. His people need not fear 'the clouds they so much dread'. Instead, through Mordecai and Esther, they are about to experience blessings which far exceed their wildest hopes.

King Xerxes

The Hebrew form of this name is 'Ahasuerus'. 'Xerxes' is the English equivalent. The Greek translation of Esther has 'Artaxerxes', but this is unhelpful, for it is also the name of another king. The king referred to in Esther is Xerxes I, the fourth king of the Persian Empire. He is mentioned in Ezra 4:6 (and is clearly distinguished from Artaxerxes in the following verse). Xerxes is remembered for destroying Babylon in 482 BC and for his unsuccessful wars against Greece (he was finally defeated in 466). He was politically powerful and wealthy, but Jewish writers portray him as weak in character and without moral fibre. Herodotus, the Greek historian, supports this opinion by describing how Xerxes found frequent consolation in the pleasures of his harem.

Wanted: a new queen

Xerxes wants a new, beautiful queen. Esther meets the criteria and becomes queen.

Entering a beauty contest must involve a great deal of preparation: months of planning, effort and probably expense as well. But would the effort be worth it? You might receive acclaim and admiration. But would you really feel valued? Would you really like to be judged purely on your looks? It has always seemed crazy to me that people are prepared to be evaluated on the basis of outward beauty, which is such a fleeting thing. Some of us take a lot of consolation from the fact that God looks at the heart (1 Samuel 16:7)!

But in these verses Esther, the heroine of our story, submits herself to a process that decides her future on the basis of what she looks like. It is unlikely that she had any choice in this, which explains why she seems blameless and untarnished despite the circumstances she finds herself in. She is described in positive terms. The writer repeats that she 'won favour' despite the foolishness of the policy to which she is subjected.

The search begins

Verses 1–4 explain the consequences of the king's edict in chapter 1. Again there is irony, because although the chapter opens with King Xerxes, it is his advisors who take the initiative to replace Queen Vashti. Verse 1 even allows us to think that Xerxes is uncomfortable with his angry actions against Vashti. (The idea of remembering is often used to convey a sense of compassion; compare God's compassion when he remembers, for example, Noah [Genesis 8:1]; Abraham and Lot [Genesis 19:29]; Hannah [1 Samuel 1:19].) If Xerxes' regret at having made the decree does prompt him to feel compassion for Vashti, he is certainly not allowed to dwell on it. His attendants quickly decide that a beautiful young woman must be found for him. It is difficult to tell whether the queen is expected to have any ruling power or whether she is to serve the king purely as an object of his desire. If the latter is the case, the emphasis on looks in this male, egotistical environment is easily explained. (Whatever the expectations, it seems that Esther could indeed exercise some authority. At least, she seems to have secured Mordecai an important position; 2:21.)

Just as Xerxes' advisors initiated the decree, so now they initiate the search for a new queen and decide the criteria by which she is to be selected. The apparently powerful Xerxes is in fact powerless: he tends to get carried along by everyone around him rather than taking well-planned initiatives for himself.

Esther emerges

The story is interrupted in verses 5–7 in order to give some background information about Esther. For the first time the author mentions the Jews, God's own people. Mordecai is also introduced and a shortened history of his family is given. The facts about Mordecai's family are important for two main reasons.

▶ They suggest that Mordecai has connections with the family of King Saul (compare 1 Samuel 9:1, which lists Kish as one of Saul's ancestors).

▶ They draw attention to the precarious nature of Mordecai's position by referring to the captivity his family had known. (Judah's King Jehoiachin was taken to Babylon in 597 BC; see 2 Kings 24:15.) This reminds us of the historical context of the story and prepares us for Esther's decision not to reveal her family background.

The story itself continues in verse 8. Starting with a general mention of 'many girls' (verse 8), the focus narrows to Esther by verse 16. The details in these verses portray Xerxes' administration in a very bad light. Verse 8 suggests that a large number of girls are rounded up. We get the impression that the girls are young and have no choice. They are controlled by Hegai, who seems to act like a personnel manager. The procedures outlined in verses 12–14 suggest that the girls are treated as objects rather than human beings. Each is expected to undergo extensive preparations that last at least one year. Their subsequent treatment depends solely on the whim of the king and his officials.

Verse 10 emphasizes how vulnerable the Jewish people are. Even a girl who had 'won favour' hesitated to reveal her background. There was no contact between the girls and their families, and this would bring inevitable anxiety.

Amid this negative picture, Esther somehow retains her dignity. She won the favour of Hegai (verse 9) and of everyone who saw her (verse 15). The idea occurs a third time in verse 17. Significantly, Esther does not simply find or obtain favour; she 'wins' it. The implication is that she has to work for it. It didn't fall at her feet without any effort on her part. Obviously her beauty is a factor (compare verse 7), but her humility, wisdom and quiet confidence also play their part. She is willing to embark on the 'make or break' moment of her life, following Hegai's advice (verse 15). She is also prepared to submit to her uncle's instructions (verse 10). Esther's wisdom, humility and discretion enhance her beauty.

Esther becomes queen

This lengthy, detailed selection procedure took time. Esther comes before Xerxes four years (verse 16) after the series of banquets which led to Vashti's demise. The contrast between the two women is clear (verses 17–18):

▶ Vashti would not come before the king. Esther did come.

▶ Vashti made Xerxes furious. Esther 'won his favour and approval'.

▶ Vashti had hosted her own banquet. Xerxes makes Esther the focus of a banquet he hosts himself.

All these facts reverse the situation described in chapter 1. The world of the king and the world of the queen are no longer poles apart. The fact that a holiday (which could mean release from taxes) and gifts (probably food) are bestowed on everyone, suggests that this union of king and queen is of great benefit to all the king's subjects. This picture of liberal giving and celebration contrasts with the scene which follows.

Questions

1. How do you react to being treated like Esther? What makes you angry about Esther's life as it is described in these verses?
2. Do you know people within and outside the church who have suffered because of their family backgrounds? How has it affected them? How far should we respect people's privacy? When might there be good reasons today to be secretive about our roots?
3. Esther found herself living in a foreign environment and complying with the wishes of foreign authorities. How can believers maintain their integrity when it is threatened by the customs of other cultures?

Character names

In our study of the book of Ruth, we noticed the importance given to names in Old Testament stories (pp. 34–35). 'Mordecai' is a name that has strong connections with 'Marduk', the chief god of Babylon. As a Jewish man whose name incorporates the name of a Babylonian deity, Esther's uncle would be fully aware of the impact of foreign powers on his people's history.

'Esther' is a Persian name that seems to be connected to the word for 'star'. Her Jewish name 'Hadassah' is the word for 'myrtle'.

Esther 2:19–23

Saved: the king's life

Esther and Mordecai foil an assassination attempt on the king.

Now Esther is in place. Somehow, through the contrivance of the Persian court, the right person is in the right place at the right time. Surely this is what we mean when we say that God works in mysterious ways. In this instance God's people, Mordecai and Esther, are in a position to protect the king from disaster. Ruth and Naomi found themselves in a similar position; they were in the right place at the right time to receive Boaz's favour, and we saw that this was acknowledged as the providence of God. In view of the unlikely circumstances that have come together for Esther, the point is obvious. Even though much of what has happened so far apparently owes its origin to the folly of a Persian king and his advisors, God is working in what is going on.

In this section we learn about one strategic event in which Esther and Mordecai were involved. Their place in Persian history is assured because they foil an assassination attempt. Although verses 19–23 are a bit short on detail, they give important insight into the personalities of Esther and Mordecai.

Esther is commended

This short paragraph continues to commend Esther's attractive qualities. Although she is now queen, she is still loyal to her uncle Mordecai. She accepts and respects his advice (verse 20). Once more, similarities to Ruth are evident. Ruth was prepared to follow the advice of her mother-in-law Naomi (see p. 52). The Bible views openness to advice as wisdom (see Proverbs 11:14; 12:15; 13:10; 19:20). The writer wants us to think of Esther as a wise person.

But her taking Mordecai's advice also says something about the nature of the relationship between them. There is a history to their friendship. Mordecai showed his love and concern for Esther 'when he was bringing her up' (verse 20) and now there is something special between them. Perhaps Proverbs 27:9 describes it well: 'the pleasantness of one's friend springs from his earnest counsel'. Years of experiencing Mordecai's sincere advice have created a truly pleasant friendship based on trust and respect. It is not surprising therefore that they can work together as a team. Together they serve the interests of the Jewish community as well as the interests of King Xerxes as their loyalty to him becomes evident. Through co-operating, they foil an attempt on the king's life (verse 22).

The final phrase in verse 22 is significant. Esther is eager to give the credit to Mordecai. Her acknowledgment of him

▶ shows that Esther's own position before the king is secure;

▶ indicates that she is quick to seize the opportunity to highlight Mordecai's loyalty; and

▶ reflects her integrity; she did not want to take the credit for something she hadn't achieved alone.

Mordecai's loyalty emerges

The emergence of the loyal Mordecai provides the backcloth to the events in the rest of the book. We see his increasing importance. Verses 19 and 21 may hint that Mordecai served as a magistrate or judge for the king. Certainly 'sitting' has overtones of presiding at a court. If this is the case, Mordecai has worked himself into an important position within the empire. Perhaps we should have expected such an event in the light of his family history (see 2:5–6). Conversely, the reference to Mordecai sitting at the king's gate may simply tell us that Mordecai is where the action is. As we have seen, the city gate was where legal and business transactions took place. Legal decisions were taken there. It was the centre of community life and gossip. If a conspiracy was emerging, this was where you would hear about it. Since Mordecai seems to have had no problem in getting messages to Esther (verse 22), perhaps the note about his whereabouts simply indicates that the lines of communication between Esther and Mordecai are still open.

The conspiracy originates with two of the king's most trusted officials, Bigthana and Teresh. As guardians of the king's doorway, they were the final line of protection for the king inside his royal palace. We are left mystified about the details of their plan. We do not know why they were angry with the king or how they planned to kill him. It is as if these details are immaterial to the writer of the story. The important fact is that their extreme disloyalty highlights Mordecai's loyalty, so that the accusations levelled against him in chapter 3 (see verse 3) are severely undermined.

Mordecai and Esther have acted honourably and wisely, but this is forgotten in the events of chapter 3. However, because the record has been written, the hope remains that honourable and wise purposes will triumph.

Questions

1. In what ways were Esther and Mordecai 'in' the Persian world but 'not of it' (see John 17:11, 14)? How can we copy their example in our world?
2. Mordecai and Esther emerge as community leaders. What characteristics do they share with leaders in your church community? What makes a good leader? How can we spot a leader emerging in our church?
3. Why are assassination attempts so cataclysmic in a nation's history? Think about the historical, political, practical and moral consequences.

GOD WANTS HIS PEOPLE TO STAND UP AND BE COUNTED

Esther 3 – 4

Stop and look

The Bible is full of incidents where God's people have to be courageous together. God's people were often an oppressed minority, and the Old Testament tells of their courageous faith and action in testing circumstances. The focus often falls upon individuals who must take on onerous responsibilities in challenging situations. When Moses encountered God's character and purpose, this shepherd's ordinary day was transformed into a crisis of life and faith (Exodus 3). Was it enough to convince him to leave the sheep and face Pharaoh? Moses needed a lot of convincing. Eventually, when he was eighty, he 'went to Pharaoh and did just as the LORD commanded' (Exodus 7:6, 10). Under his leadership, God's people were finally released from Egyptian slavery. Although he was old and lacked eloquence, this man was the person God chose to stand up and be counted, to take courage and to act.

But his achievements were not his own. The exodus story is full of reminders that God will stretch out his arm and redeem his people (for example, Exodus 6:6–8). When God tells someone to stand up and be counted, he does not leave him or her alone to do it. Instead, he comes as the great 'I AM' (see Exodus 3:14), the present one, whose power can never be overcome by the greatest human strength.

The experience of Moses is the experience of Joshua, David, Isaiah, Jeremiah, Mordecai and of course Esther – to name but a few. As God's people face pressure, individuals' actions point to God's ultimate power and glory. Moments of crisis reveal people's character and faith; they lose sight of themselves and their weaknesses, and their external circumstances, however oppressive, become opportunities to work hand in hand with God.

Esther 3 shows us Mordecai's courage despite the great evil represented by Haman. In chapter 4 Esther struggles to respond to the challenge, to trust and to obey. These two chapters present us with a man and a woman who are uniquely placed to work for God and his people. Their faith and courage have never been forgotten. Who knows? If we too co-operate with God like this, something momentous might happen – something that might be worth celebrating for years to come (as Esther's actions were in the festival of Purim), and even for eternity.

Esther 3:1–6

Whom should I honour?

Mordecai refuses to respect Haman. Haman's anger against Mordecai leads him to attempt to destroy the whole Jewish nation.

Where does evil come from? These verses give us a few clues. They warn us against the perils of high position and the pride and arrogance that so often can accompany it. Haman is consumed by his own status. The lack of respect shown by one Jewish man is enough to provoke him to devise an evil plan against a whole nation. How do such extremes of evil and resentment gain a hold? Perhaps we should not be surprised at the injustice of Haman's plan. The Bible tells us that evil people 'do not understand justice' (Proverbs 28:5). Perhaps Proverbs 30:32–33 explains the inevitability of Haman's evil intent: 'If you have played the fool and exalted yourself, or if you have planned evil, clap your hand over your mouth! For as churning the milk produces butter, and as twisting the nose produces blood, so stirring up anger produces strife.' As soon as Haman begins to vent his anger, lies pour out of his mouth. The result is strife, bewilderment and mourning for God's people. It seems to me that Haman's evil intent came from the pride and anger of his heart. The events recorded in chapter 3 are a vivid demonstration of James's words, 'Everyone should be ... slow to become angry, for man's human anger does not bring about the righteous life that God desires' (James 1:19–20).

'I won't conform'

Verses 1–4 explain why Haman was angry with Mordecai. Mordecai does not comply with the king's command to honour Haman. We don't know why Mordecai stubbornly refuses to kneel down before Haman. Was he just being arrogant or petty? Perhaps he expected high position and honour himself – after all, he had uncovered the conspiracy against the king (2:21–23). It does seem shocking that when Esther gives credit to Mordecai before the king (2:22), the next thing we hear is that the king elevates Haman! The royal officials think Mordecai's actions may amount to civil disobedience.

Perhaps their hesitation (along with the details in verses 1 and 4) suggests that there is a history to the conflict between Haman and Mordecai which makes the latter's action a matter of principle. Verse 1 explains that Haman is the son of 'the Agagite'. This is probably a reference to the Agag who was king of the Amalekites in Saul's time (1 Samuel 15:20). The Amalekites were the enemies of God's people. So by refusing to honour Haman, Mordecai is refusing to kneel before a descendant of the Amalekites. This makes sense of verse 6, which hints that Mordecai's refusal to honour Haman has something to do with his Jewish identity. God's people were told to 'Remember what the Amalekites did to you ... you shall blot out the memory of Amalek from under heaven' (Deuteronomy 25:17–19). Perhaps Mordecai realizes that kneeling before Haman would perpetuate Amalek's memory, not blot it out, and therefore is incompatible with his faith. We can imagine the likely outcome of such nonconformity; Vashti was deposed for refusing to come (1:12). Surely Mordecai would also be punished. Nevertheless, he is prepared to stand up and be counted, and in this way he anticipates the courage required of Esther.

'I'll show him!'

Haman's response to finding out about Mordecai's non-compliance, which he takes as a personal affront, is callous rage (verses 5–6). His anger against Mordecai turns into senseless hatred for the whole Jewish nation. Just as Mordecai seems to have understood Haman as a representative of the Amalekites, so Haman sees Mordecai as a representative of his own people group. Mordecai stirs up intense feelings of rivalry between these old enemies. But these two men are described in very different ways. Mordecai, it seems, makes a calm, considered protest. Haman demands widespread killing, and looks for a way to achieve it. He behaves like foolish Xerxes, who 'burned with anger' (1:12). Both Mordecai and Haman are prepared to act to support their cause. The difference is that Mordecai's cause is God's cause; Haman's cause is himself.

Questions

1. Think of a recent incident when your pride was hurt. Why did it happen? How did you feel and react?
2. In church life, what causes do we take up? How can we assess whether they reflect our own interests, God's interests, or the interests of others?
3. Is Mordecai's non-compliance to be admired? Why? How might upholding Christian principles put us out of line with the way our society expects people to behave? What examples can you think of? What were the consequences?

Esther 3:7–15

'Do what you like'

Haman persuades Xerxes to support his plan to destroy the Jews.

The striking feature about these verses is the indifference that Xerxes shows towards Haman's plans. It is one thing to consult officials about Vashti's fate and to go along with their advice (chapter 1), but to sanction Haman's plans to destroy a whole people group and then to sit down to drink (3:15) is incredible. Now the moral integrity, and even the sanity, of Xerxes is questioned. There is still a level of irony in the story (Xerxes is king in name but nothing in practice), but there is no longer any humour. A king who says 'Do as you like' to someone like Haman is dangerous. These verses seem designed to increase the tension. The situation is volatile, unpredictable and out of control. Evil intentions are gaining the upper hand, because even the king has succumbed to them.

Lies and bribes

Haman is keen to ensure that he has luck on his side before he presents his plan to Xerxes. He casts lots to decide when his plan should be put into action (verse 7), and then speaks to the king (verses 8–9).

He doesn't mention the Jews by name, but refers to them as 'a certain people'. Perhaps he thinks his own integrity might be questioned if Mordecai the Jew, who had after all uncovered the conspiracy against Xerxes (2:19–23), came to the king's mind. How could Haman claim that 'it is not in the king's best interests to tolerate' him (verse 8)?

Haman mixes truth, half-truths and lies to create a negative impression of the Jewish people. He describes them as a threat to Xerxes and as social misfits. He suggests that, being scattered, they enjoy widespread influence, and that they practise customs 'different from those of all other people'. The truth is that the Jews did have different customs. The half-truth is the sweeping generalization that they 'do not obey the king's laws' (verse 8). (The only evidence we have in the story is that one Jewish man, Mordecai, disobeys one of the king's commands. Even the officials were unsure how serious this act of defiance was; 3:3–4.) The lie is that tolerating the Jews is 'not in the king's best interests'.

Thus Haman dishonestly creates a false impression and inflames prejudice. He lacks integrity, and is even willing to offer Xerxes a huge bribe to get what he wants (verse 9). Haman sees no way to deal with the Jews but to destroy them, a solution immediately accepted by Xerxes without further questioning or reflection. Again Xerxes avoids the trouble of thinking by simply agreeing. He gives Haman his signet ring, the sign of his authority. In effect, Xerxes hands over his power to Haman. Haman can now seal any decree and have it recognized throughout the empire. He really can do whatever he wants. In deed as well as in word he can prove himself to be 'the enemy of the Jews' (verse 10).

Sealed and sent out

The speed of the operation is captured by verses 12–15. The decree is issued in every language and script necessary. The royal secretaries, satraps, governors, nobles and couriers are all involved. The decree specifies that every Jew (even 'young and old, women and little children') is to be destroyed on 'the thirteenth day of the twelfth month, the month of Adar', and their goods are to be plundered. It would be as if the Jews had never existed. An eleven-month delay is envisaged between the writing of the decree (verse 12) and the day it would be carried out (verse 13). This gives the reader a glimmer of hope. We know that Esther and

Mordecai have *time* to do something, but do they have the *ability* to undo what has been sealed and widely disseminated? The odds seem stacked against them.

Two further facts emerge:

▶ The king and Haman sit down content as if their desire to destroy the Jews has already been achieved – but it hasn't.

▶ Haman summons the royal secretaries on the day before the Jews would have killed the lambs for the Passover (see Exodus 12:6). Passover is a time of hope for the Jews, as they celebrate how God had delivered them from the oppression of Pharaoh in Egypt.

Despite the bewilderment in the city of Susa (verse 15), there is still reason for hope. It is centred on a heavenly King who, in stark contrast to Xerxes, has always protected his people and always will. The God of the Jews will never say to any official, however great or weak, 'Do what you like.'

Questions

1. Why is it so easy to slander people by our words? Read James 3:1–12. Perhaps you could spend time in silent prayer, asking God for forgiveness for slanderous words, and for integrity of speech.
2. What should distinguish God's people from those around us? What in fact distinguishes us from them, if anything? Which of these things reflect God's character, and which of them put people off unnecessarily?
3. Do Haman's words in verse 8 amount to racism? Why? Can you think of typical modern-day racist comments that involve generalizations? What are the flaws and perils in generalizing about groups of people? How can we recognize and deal with our own racist tendencies?

'Keep the money'

It is unclear from the text whether Xerxes was guilty or not guilty of being enticed by the bribe. 'Keep the money' (3:11) is literally, 'The silver is given to you.' Perhaps Xerxes was bargaining over the amount of money. Or perhaps he was saying that the money in the treasury was now at Haman's disposal as he pursued his plan against the Jews.

The Jewish calendar

Understanding the references to the months and days in this chapter is not straightforward. The Hebrew text of verse 7 is unclear, although it does seem to indicate that Haman (and company) cast lots to determine precisely when the destruction of the Jews should take place. The lots were cast in the first month, Nisan, and on 13 Nisan the secretaries were summoned (verse 12). The decree said that the Jews should be destroyed on the thirteenth day of the twelfth month, Adar (verse 13). Ironically, the number thirteen was considered unlucky to the Babylonians and Persians, while for the Jews the month of Nisan was the time of their joyous Passover celebrations. Moreover, the month of Adar, when the destruction was due to take place, was to become marked by another great festival of deliverance, Purim (see chapter 9).

Number of month	Name of month	Modern calendar equivalents	Festivals
1	Abib-Nisan	March – April	Passover, Unleavened Bread, Firstfruits
2	Ziv	April–May	
3	Sivan	May–June	Pentecost (Weeks)
4	Tammuz	June–July	
5	Ab	July–August	
6	Elul	August–September	
7	Ethanim	September–October	Trumpets, Atonement, Tabernacles (Booths)
8	Bul	October–November	
9	Kislev	November–December	Hannukah (Dedication)
10	Tebeth	December–January	
11	Shebat	January–February	
12	Adar	February–March	Purim

Bad news travels fast

God's people are grief-stricken, but as Esther enters the story again, so does hope.

 If there is one thing that travels faster than good news, it is bad news. Perhaps it's because of our pessimistic nature, or because bad news often makes a powerful story. Here in Esther the news of crisis for God's people travels fast. The bewilderment at the end of chapter 3 gives way to shared and public distress in chapter 4. Staring death in the face, Mordecai urges Esther to align herself with her people by begging for mercy.

Mourning, fasting, weeping and wailing

Verses 1–5 match the all-inclusive scope of 3:13. The decree had ordered the death of every Jew without exception. Now in 'every province' there is 'great mourning'. The chapter begins with Mordecai, who typifies the Jewish response and again represents his people.

The people fast (verse 3) as part of their public display of distress. The contrast is stark between the flamboyant feasting of the Persian court and the lot of the Jewish subjects, for whom feasting is the last thing on their minds.

Fasting is one of the key features of Jewish faith, and accompanies prayer. The fact that the Jews are driven to fasting means they are driven to God and to prayer. (Think of Daniel's prayer, mourning and fasting in Daniel 9:1–17.) God is not absent from this story. He is the key to understanding the words and actions of his people. In fact, all the different ways of mourning expressed here are associated with seeking mercy from God. The Jews are certain about their need for that!

Mordecai's reaction to the decree is public and demonstrative. Tearing clothes and lying in sackcloth and ashes shows intense emotion in mourning (Genesis 37:34–35; 2 Samuel 1:11–12; Daniel 9:3). Perhaps Mordecai felt particularly responsible, because he was the one who had provoked Haman. (Verse 7 supports this: Mordecai begins to explain his grief by recounting 'everything that had happened to him'.) Perhaps Mordecai was particularly distressed about the way Xerxes had been bribed into making the decree (as mentioned in his report to Hathach; verse 7). But maybe Mordecai's demonstration of grief is simply to gain Esther's attention. It certainly does so, even though she learns of it through maids and eunuchs and Hathach.

At first, Esther reacts to Mordecai's mourning and not to the decree itself; indeed, she seems ignorant of the decree (verses 4–5). Her anxiety may be heightened because she is unaware of the reason for Mordecai's grief. Though some condemn her reaction as impetuous or superficial, she is eager to find out what is troubling her uncle. She sends him clothes so that he can go through the king's gate again (compare verse 2). This would at least increase Esther's chances of finding out what the trouble is. But Mordecai is not easily persuaded to end his open demonstration of grief. Persistent as ever, Esther sends Hathach, who proves to be a most reliable messenger. The king is surrounded by unreliable servants, but Esther's attendants are loyal, efficient and trustworthy.

Telling it as it is ...

First Mordecai speaks with Hathach (verses 7–8), and then Hathach speaks with Esther (verse 9). The conversation between Mordecai and Hathach is

▶ public (verse 6);

▶ accurate; Mordecai does not elaborate the story for effect;

▶ informed; somehow Mordecai even knows about the money Haman had promised Xerxes;

▶ credible; Mordecai provides information to support his report about Haman's plans;

▶ determined; Mordecai knows that Esther can help. This is the last time he tells her what she should do, but this time her co-operation is more critical than ever;

▶ urgent; Mordecai tells Hathach to 'urge' Esther to 'plead' for her people. We are simply told that he 'went back' and 'reported' to Esther without any details (verse 9).

In circumstances like these there is no point in beating about the bush. In a crisis, plain, honest and urgent speech is called for.

Questions

1. How do you respond to a crisis? How can we decide when to keep quiet, when to speak out and when to act?
2. Why should, or shouldn't the Christian church fast today? What is your experience of fasting?
3. Should Christians seek to change local and national government policies? Why or why not? What policies would you like to see overturned, and why?

Fasting

In the Bible 'fasting' means abstaining from food, usually as part of a religious ritual or to demonstrate earnestness in asking God for mercy. Essentially, it is self-denial. Individuals and groups can fast, in response to leaders or out of free choice. Early in their history the Jewish people held a fast on the annual Day of Atonement, and eventually other fasts were introduced (see Leviticus 16:29–31; Zechariah 7:3; Esther 9:31). Fasting can involve any or all of the following:

▶ conviction of sin (e.g. 1 Samuel 7:6);

▶ urgent longing for deliverance (e.g. Joel 1:13–15);

▶ deep sorrow in bereavement (e.g. 2 Samuel 1:12);

▶ an urgent desire for God's guidance (e.g. 2 Chronicles 20:3).

The prophets warn against fasting which is just a duty or ritual and is not done out of right attitudes to God and others (for example, Isaiah 58:3–12). Jesus too warns against hypocritical fasting (Matthew 6:16–18). In New Testament times fasts seem to have multiplied and to have become a regular part of a religious lifestyle. Jesus does not criticize the practice (he kept a forty-day fast himself; Luke 4:2), but he does criticize those who promote fasting as an end in itself. Throughout the centuries Christians have kept fasts at times of personal and national disaster and when they desire to draw near to God in a special way. In the New Testament church, fasting is particularly associated with setting apart church leaders (see Acts 13:2–3; 14:23).

'If I perish, I perish'

Esther responds to the crisis facing God's people with personal courage and deep faith.

 Have you ever stood back and asked yourself, 'What is my life all about? How many potentially defining moments have I missed? How many times have my thoughts and concerns been so self-centred, cautious or confused that I have consciously or even subconsciously chosen not to be, or to do, God's best for me?'

In these verses Mordecai suggests to Esther that her life might well be all about one defining moment. Speaking plainly and directly, he convinces her that God has placed her where she is for a purpose. God wants to use her, but she has a choice: to be used or not. That is not in fact quite correct. Moredecai implies that Esther has no real choice at all. Circumstances dictate what she must choose, but she still has to be courageous. We need friends like Mordecai who will speak to us boldly and plainly, and we do well to respond with faith and courage like Esther.

Not me!

Esther's position is precarious (verses 10–11). It seems that her beauty had captivated the king only briefly. For a whole month the king hasn't given her a passing thought. Queen she may be, but she has no more privileges than anyone else in the royal court. She cannot presume she will escape with her life if she approaches the king without being summoned. As she hasn't been summoned for thirty days, she must be out of favour. It is hard for us to understand the set-up in the royal court at Susa, but the rules are clear to Esther. If she approaches the king without being sent for, the most likely outcome is her own death. How could Mordecai ask her to risk her life in a probably vain attempt to secure the safety of the Jewish people?

Yes, you!

Mordecai's response to Esther's protest seems harsh and heartless (verses 12–14). He seems to show no sympathy for Esther in her unenviable position. If I were Esther I would have expected Mordecai to say, 'You're right. It's foolish for you to risk your life in these circumstances. Let's think about Plan B.' Instead, Mordecai determinedly challenges Esther to look at the situation from a different perspective. He tells her two things:

▶ you are with the rest of the Jews in this; and

▶ you are in the royal household for this.

In other words, Mordecai reminds Esther that she is a Jewish queen. On the one hand, she is in as much danger as the rest of the Jews, but on the other she is in a position which might just enable her to rescue all the Jewish people including herself. Mordecai's words are inspired by faith:

▶ he believes that God's plan to rescue his people will succeed with or without Esther (verse 14a); and

▶ he believes that God has worked in Esther's life to this point precisely so that through her his people may be rescued (verse 14b).

Far from being harsh and heartless, Mordecai longs for his niece to fulfil God's purposes for her life. This will be for Esther's good: she and her family will not perish. Perhaps this means that Esther's family will be physically preserved only if she co-operates with God's plan. Perhaps Mordecai, with the forward view of faith, is suggesting that Esther's family name will be preserved and remembered if she fulfils her God-given duty at this time.

Alternatively, Mordecai's words could be translated with negative force: 'If you remain silent at this time, no relief and deliverance will arise for the Jews from any other quarter, and you and your father's house will perish.' If this is correct, it implies that Esther is the only person able to help. Understanding Mordecai's words in this way ties in with his aim to motivate Esther to do something. Since the day he adopted Esther, Mordecai has always shown his concern for her physical well-being. Now he shows concern too for her spiritual well-being, which she will preserve only though courageous action.

Yes, me!

Mordecai's words prove sufficient. Esther responds with confession, faith and action (verses 15–17). She does not ignore the threat to her life, but accepts it. The words 'If I perish, I perish' are solemn and sobering. Esther realizes that she may not survive if she goes to the king and breaks the law. She is not being fatalistic, but is taking action to increase the likelihood of her survival.

First, *she entrusts Mordecai with carrying out her instructions.* This is a key moment in the story, for it is the first time Mordecai takes instructions from Esther. It is as if he has prepared her all her life for this moment of initiative, leadership and authority. He is the first to recognize the importance of following her lead.

Secondly, *she asks all the Jews in Susa to hold a fast for her* (verse 16). Esther's commitment involves enlisting the support of the people. Her humility and wisdom are clear. She recognizes the critical nature of her plans, and is eager and willing to seek support among God's people.

Thirdly, *she commits herself (and her maids) to fast too.* She thus identifies herself with her people just as Mordecai suggested she should (verse 12). By fasting, she accepts her personal responsibility and confesses her reliance on God.

The fast is to be exceptionally long and severe. Usually a

day's fast involved not taking food from sunrise to sunset. Here the fast is to last three days and nights and includes abstaining from drink as well as food. We have already noted how fasting is connected to prayer in the Old Testament. Prayer is not mentioned here, but it is implied. The people fast on Esther's behalf ('for me', verse 16), and is therefore a kind of intercession. Esther's fasting (and that of her maids) may also have had this character, but she is probably expressing her need for God's presence, protection and wisdom as she commits herself to the task in hand. We have noted (see p. 112) that fasting shows a desire to draw close to God and to receive his guidance.

So Esther assumes the mantle of responsibility. She is prepared to stand up and be counted as one of God's people for the sake of God's people. The consequences may be fatal. But with the tangible support of God's people, expressed through their fast on her behalf, she prepares herself for the action which her royal position obliges her to undertake.

Questions

1. What does it mean to you that God has a purpose for you and that you can play a part in that purpose? Think whether there is any situation now where only you can make a difference or change things around. What action will you take?

2. How willing are you to receive advice and support from other Christians? Have you a special friend, relative or advisor, as Esther had in Mordecai? How do you respond to hard and challenging advice from this person? Do you ever ask your church to pray for you and support you? If not, why not? If you do, what differences does it make?

3. Esther decided to go to the king 'even though it is against the law' (verse 16). When, if ever, is it right to break our country's laws? What are the arguments for and against such an idea?

3

GOD HONOURS
FAITHFUL PEOPLE

Esther 5 – 6

Stop and look

One key word in the book of Esther as a whole, and particularly in chapters 5 – 6, is 'honour'. It is difficult to replace this rather old-fashioned word with a more modern-sounding one. It has several meanings and connotations. We talk about children honouring their parents and even parents honouring their children. People are honoured because of their achievements, personal, commercial or political. Schools and colleges honour the achievements of pupils and staff. In the church, we talk about honouring God, one another and ourselves. In all these cases honour has to do with respecting and valuing people and their achievements.

In the book of Esther we are introduced to the idea when the king decrees that all women must honour (respect) their husbands (1:20). Later, the king honours Haman by promoting him (3:1). Mordecai, however, refuses to show respect to Haman (3:2, 5), while Xerxes continues to confer respect and honour on him (verse 10). Chapters 5 – 6 also focus on the theme. But first, chapter 4 has intervened. There is nothing about honour there. Rather, the writer stresses the absence of value, worth and dignity. The Jews, including Esther, are well aware that they are not held in honour. No-one values even their lives, let alone their achievements. In chapters 5 – 6 their position begins to be reversed. The king honours Esther by extending his sceptre to her, and Mordecai is repeatedly referred to as 'the man the king delights to honour' (6:6, 9, 11). Having lost all honour, Haman is put to death for his evil intentions (chapter 7). Finally, in chapter 8 the Jews are described as a people who together enjoy 'happiness and joy, gladness and honour' (verse 16). The chief example of their new status is Mordecai, who is promoted ('raised') by the king to an eminent position and held in high esteem.

The book of Esther shows us that God honours his people, because he values the lives of the people he has called his own. Because he loves them, he desires their honour. The story of Esther vividly illustrates his words through Isaiah: 'Since you are precious and honoured in my sight, and because I love you, I will give men in exchange for you' (Isaiah 43:4). There is such an exchange in Esther's story: Haman loses his honour as the Jews gain theirs. Isaiah portrays a servant of God whose honour is stripped away because he bears the dishonour of others. As he sacrifices his life in this way, the will of the Lord prospers (Isaiah 53:10), because the Lord honours those who serve him (John 12:26).

The startling truth is that the honour God confers on his people often follows shame and disgrace. In this, Jesus is our example and inspiration: 'We see Jesus, who was made a little lower than the angels, now crowned with glory and honour because he suffered death, so that by the grace of God he might taste death for everyone' (Hebrews 2:9).

Esther 5:1–8

Anything to please

Esther speaks with the king and invites him, along with Haman, to two banquets.

Are you good at putting off today whatever can be done tomorrow? I'm an expert. I leave the ironing for days. I try not to use our car when it needs filling up with petrol. I don't get round to making my next appointment at the dentist. Paperwork piles up in my kitchen, although there's a perfectly good filing cabinet upstairs. I don't deliberately decide to neglect the ironing, the petrol tank, the dentist and the filing. I just don't seem to get round to them.

At other times, I have reason to delay. I may sit on an invitation for a few days to see how other plans work out. I may wait for the right opportunity to talk with someone about a concern I have or an encouraging comment I want to pass on. A difficult letter might sit on my desk for a few days before I send it.

Surprisingly, Esther seems to procrastinate here. She has already given herself a three-day space before she meets the king. Now that she has the chance to beg him for mercy for the Jews, she delays even more. She invites the king to a banquet, and then to another on the following day. We may be tempted to blame Esther for losing her nerve and prolonging the risk for the Jewish people. But chapters 5 – 6 level no such criticism at her. She appears to wait calmly for the very best moment to open her heart to Xerxes. In fact, by the time she does so (chapter 7), he has already promised to give Esther anything she wants. She has won his favour and he has enjoyed two banquets. In addition, of course, the king has, of his own volition, publicly declared his gratitude to Mordecai (who remains representative of the Jewish people). Because Esther realizes what a critical role she has, she knows that her every move is important. She delays, but for good reason. In the meantime she makes every effort to please the king, and he responds by wanting to please her.

Royal robes

Esther prepares carefully to approach the king. First, she puts on her royal robes (verse 1). The text literally reads, 'Esther put on royalty.' This suggests that she is doing more than simply putting on garments. She is accepting her royal position (verse 1 uses the same expression as in 4:14). Her royal robes are literally and symbolically important. By putting them on, Esther is accepting God's call as well as preparing herself properly to stand before the king.

Secondly, she stands in the inner court of the palace (verse 1). She does not presume to enter the throne room. Instead, she waits in the wings to see what response the king will give her.

Finally, she wins the king's favour (verse 8). Once more the story-writer expresses this in an active rather than a passive way (compare 2:15, 17). The favour Esther receives does not come her way by chance; she has to work for it. She looks beautiful, but behaves with humility. Her life is preserved because the king extends his gold sceptre to her, but Esther had more than a little to do with her own preservation.

The king confers further dignity on Esther. He calls her 'Queen Esther', as if he delights in her royalty (verse 3). He seems aware that Esther must have a special request, and is prepared to commit himself to do absolutely anything for her. The repeated promise 'even up to half the kingdom' (verses 3, 6) is best understood as an indication of the king's goodwill to Esther rather than as a literal offer.

It is interesting to see how Esther takes control of events (verses 4–8). She is now clothed not only in robes but also in authority. At the end of chapter 4 she gave instructions to Mordecai. Now she gives instructions (politely, of course) to the king and his deputy. So the king and Haman come to her banquet. Roles have been reversed; in chapter 1 Vashti was called to the king's banquet and wouldn't come. Now the replacement queen is issuing the invitation, and the king is willing to come straight away (verse 5).

The drama is further heightened by the fact that she invites Haman to her banquet. Haman counts this an honour (verse 12), and we become a little disturbed at good Esther's conferring honour on evil Haman. At the same time we are full of hope. We anticipate that she will be able to achieve further remarkable things. For somehow, by the time we reach verse 8, Esther has convinced the king that he will be pleased to do what she requests even before she made the request. Far from procrastinating, Esther has carefully devised stage one of her plan. She has worked to gain the king's pleasure, and now he is happy to please her in turn.

Questions

---

1. What personal qualities of Esther's would we do well to copy? Which of them specially apply to a situation you are facing now?
2. The Bible often portrays God as a king (e.g. Psalms 47:2, 7–8; 145:1, 11–13), and Jesus came proclaiming the kingdom (or reign) of God (e.g. Mark 1:15; Luke 4:43). What does this picture tell us about God? How then should we approach him, both in our own prayer times and in church worship? Unlike Esther, how can we be sure our King will 'hold out his sceptre' to us?
3. 'Don't put off until tomorrow what you can do today.' Is this always good advice? What issues does the world face today which require us to plan solutions carefully, without rushing in?

Esther 5:9–14

Happy but haunted

Haman demonstrates his volatile character. His personal anger leads him to accept his wife's advice to hang Mordecai.

The destructive power of personal bitterness and anger is evident in these verses. Haman almost gains our pity, because we see how pathetic and pointless  life is for a person who is consumed by rage and evil intent. In contrast to Esther, Haman is controlled, not controlling. Even fleeting happiness is haunted by the scorn which wells up in his heart. Sometimes we think that we can enjoy life whatever our attitude towards ourselves or towards other people. These few verses confront us with the consequences of egocentric pride.

Happy

The phrase 'happy and in high spirits' (verse 9) connects Haman's sense of happiness with that of King Xerxes in 1:10. 'High spirits' is used in both passages, but in 1:10 Xerxes' state of mind resulted from drinking wine. Esther's banquet also included a wine-drinking session (5:6), and it is clear that Haman's happiness is superficial and transient. The word 'happy' is frequently found in passages describing merriment that comes by drink. It also conveys the idea of gloating. By using these two expressions the writer emphasizes that Haman's happiness is in fact his foolishness. He has no idea why Esther is hosting the banquets, so when he is invited he boasts about it to his friends and his wife (verse 12). Ironically, Zeresh's proposal to erect a stake for Mordecai is meant to ensure that Haman has a good time at the next banquet (verse 14). Zeresh does not claim that getting rid of Mordecai will bring Haman lasting joy and happiness. At best, it will only bring a moment of merriment.

Zeresh's advice 'seemed good' to Haman (the NIV translation 'delighted' is a little enthusiastic). The phrase is frequently used in the Old Testament to indicate that the advice given is adequate to the situation. Does this mean that Zeresh's advice, rather than delighting Haman, was just the best idea either of them could come up with?

Haunted

There is as much about lack of happiness as there is about merriment here. Haman perceives that his problems begin and end with Mordecai. He is frustrated that one man can take away all his satisfaction (verse 13). Haman simply cannot stand the sight of Mordecai: he is an insult to his pride (verse 9; see also chapter 3). Despite the events of the intervening chapters, Moredecai is still sitting at the king's gate among the king's officials (compare 3:2). So no-one else has taken steps to remove the Jew. His actions, an affront to Haman, are apparently of little significance to everyone else.

This adds to Haman's frustration and anger. But he controls his temper (verse 10). Perhaps he realizes that venting his anger would have done his reputation no good at all. Perhaps he consoles himself with the thought that Mordecai and his people would soon be gone. Perhaps he is counting the days until the edict against the Jews would be implemented. Perhaps he is eager to get back to his friends and wife and share his good fortune with them. Whatever the truth, Haman seems to be confronting a problem within himself. He refrains from acting (verse 10), but he can't help mentioning Mordecai's name again and expressing his disdain for him (verse 13).

Haman's weakness is the egocentricity that swells his pride. The irony is that, just as in Xerxes' case in chapter 1, his weakness is exposed by his wife. Zeresh takes over. She tells Haman what to do, and he complies. The size of the gallows represents his enormous desire for Mordecai to be publicly disgraced. Only this would satisfy Haman's search for revenge and personal acclaim.

Questions

1. Make two columns on a sheet of paper. On one side, list the characteristics of Esther which emerge in this chapter. On the other, list the characteristics of Haman. How do they contrast with each other? Why do we often find ourselves conforming to the example of Haman? How might we remedy our failings and become more like Esther?

2. How do you react to receiving invitations, or to *not* being invited to things? How much does 'honour' from other people matter to you? Is there anyone you 'can't stand the sight of'? Why has this bitterness taken hold of you,

and how can you deal with it?

3. What lessons can we learn about leadership and authority from the details of the Persian court that we have seen so far in Esther? Which governments in the world today reflect the attitudes of the Persian leadership and administration? Which contrast with them?

Esther 6:1–14

In royal robes

Haman's plans meet God's plans head on. Mordecai is honoured and Haman is grief-stricken.

 If you want to know what the pride that comes before a fall looks like and feels like, search no further than this chapter. The irony is clear: Haman expects honour (verse 6) but receives disgrace. Far from instigating actions, he is now on the receiving end of the actions of others. He is stopped in his tracks. Events and circumstances overpower his own plans, and even his closest allies admit that there is a mysterious 'religious' element at work here (verse 13). The story is shaped around a series of coincidences:

► the king can't sleep;

► the account of the conspiracy against Xerxes is read to him;

► Haman enters the court on cue.

Haman's own machinations meet a higher authority. He

and all his plans are just pawns in a heavenly game. His plans have dominated proceedings thus far, but the tables are being turned.

Honour is forgotten

Verses 1–6 show us a side of Xerxes' character that has been less clearly seen until now. Here Xerxes seems naturally disposed towards fairness. He is keen to reward loyal and faithful people. He recognizes that Mordecai has never received any reward for saving the king's life and he takes steps to ensure that this oversight is corrected. The question in verse 3 is rather surprising. Surely the king would himself know that Mordecai had received no particular recognition. Perhaps he was just checking with his attendants out of courtesy towards those who seem to have controlled operations until this point. Perhaps he is rebuking them for their inactivity on this matter. Xerxes' questions continue: he wants to know who has entered the outer court. For once Xerxes seems to have the bit between his teeth. He knows he must sort out the issue of Mordecai's honour, so he summons Haman and immediately asks him what he should do to honour someone. The irony is great: Haman arrives thinking of the gallows; the king wants to bestow honour. But both are thinking of Mordecai.

Honour is demonstrated

It is Haman who suggests the package of honour described in verses 7–9. The man to be honoured should

- wear a royal robe that the king has worn;

- ride a horse, with a royal crest, that the king has ridden;

- be attended by one of the king's most noble princes, namely Haman himself; and

- receive public honour.

The package Haman suggests in fact exalts this man as equal to the king. The parade is centred on one man. The king takes no part. Only a Haman could conceive this package, because it is characterized by the egocentricity that is the hallmark of his life. It is startling then to find that Mordecai is at its centre. Afterwards, he simply returns to his usual position at the king's gate (verse 12). In contrast, Haman, who so craves public recognition, is reduced to tears (verse 12). Even though he has performed the role of 'one of the king's most noble princes', he feels despised. Someone who craves all the honour cannot bear to see someone else receive acclaim.

What makes the events in this chapter so realistic is the portrayal of the all-consuming nature of human pride and arrogance. In the end, 'A man's pride brings him low.' But what makes this chapter so striking is that 'a man of lowly spirit gains honour' (Proverbs 29:23). But the honour given to Mordecai here is only a foretaste of that which is to come to him and to God's people. Mordecai was to get to wear the royal robes (and a crown) again, and his honour, with that of the Jewish people, was going to be both celebrated and feared (Esther 8:15–17).

Honour is absent

The final verses of the chapter serve to set in motion Haman's downfall. As Haman grieves his loss of honour, his wife and friends confirm the gloom. They had been the ones to suggest the gallows for Mordecai (5:14), but now they lay the responsibility and the consequences on Haman alone. In chapter 3, being Jewish meant the death sentence; now being Jewish means victory over ruined enemies (verse 13). Haman is losing control as God and his people take control. Even as Haman is receiving his depressing counsel, he is rushed off to the banquet Esther has arranged. He is losing his dignity, and, being without honour, his future is uncertain.

Questions

1. Try to imagine how it would have felt to be in Mordecai's shoes. How would he have felt at being led out by Haman? Why?
2. What place does applause and public recognition have in church life? What are the positive and negative effects?
3. Can you think of situations in the world today where evil purposes have seemed to meet God's purposes head on? What happened? What role does coincidence play in world events?

4

GOD TURNS THE TABLES

Esther 7 – 8

Do you remember the crisis in Kosovo? Our televisions showed us ethnic Albanians weeping and wailing as they suffered under a regime committed to their annihilation. Their experience recalls the helpless despair of the Jews in Esther 4:1–3. Later, we saw rejoicing and celebration in Kosovo as the refugees returned home and their survival seemed possible. There was a turnaround of fortunes similar to that which the Jews anticipated as the events of Esther 7 – 8 unfolded. But how did the Kosovan situation develop? We saw new refugees wailing and weeping: Serbian people were now leaving their homes and fleeing for their lives. They began to suffer the pain which the ethnic Albanians had experienced at Serbian hands. They were loaded on to similar tractors with a similar lack of dignity and with apparent hopelessness. Again this is mirrored by the Esther story, particularly in chapters 7 – 8. The transition of God's people from being victims to being victors, from shame to unrivalled honour, requires the public humiliation of her enemies. The joy of God's people is intrinsically linked to the shame and death of Haman.

This seems consistent with the divine plan of things. We see the pattern repeated throughout the Old Testament as God's people secure victories at the expense of their enemies. This pattern confirms God's commitment to justice. When he brings about a complete reversal of fortunes for his people, injustices have to be paid for, wrongs have to be made right. The cross of Christ secures the final reversal of fortunes for God's people. Our sin is paid for in Jesus' greatest moment of humiliation and shame. But God is committed to securing eternal justice. The power of sin that held Jesus to the cross is itself finally defeated through his resurrection and exaltation to the right hand of God the Father. The celebration of the Jews at the end of Esther 8 is merely a foretaste of the celebration that God's people will enjoy when God's enemies will finally be defeated as every knee bows before him. If our present circumstances convince us that we need God to turn the situation around for us, we do well to remember these words: 'If we are children, then we are heirs – heirs of God and co-heirs with Christ, if indeed we share in his sufferings in order that we may also share in his glory. I consider that our present sufferings are not worth comparing with the glory that will be revealed in us' (Romans 8:17–18).

Esther 7:1–10

Shamed!

Esther identifies Haman as her enemy. The king agrees that Haman should be hanged on the gallows he erected for Mordecai.

 This short chapter explains the process by which Haman met his ultimate downfall: his own death. In the course of the story thus far he has plotted the downfall and death of others, but now the tables are turned. Haman's shame is great because his honour had been great. His public and gruesome death fits the crime of which he is guilty. Today we frequently witness the public downfall of politicians and public figures whose honour evaporates as their misdemeanors surface. Haman's demise reminds us that the higher the perch, the further the fall. It is a salutary reminder to everyone who assumes a position of leadership and responsibility.

This chapter resembles a courtroom scene: the charge is

brought (verses 1–6) and the sentence is given (verses 7–10). Although Esther brings the charge, she plays no part in deciding or executing judgment. Her God-given role is restricted and she shows no inclination to overstep the mark.

The request for life

Esther shows herself shrewd. She is not reticent or weak, but deliberate and determined. She has her eyes on the goal, and has worked out a careful strategy to achieve her aim.

She waits for her moment. Although the text of verse 1 suggests that things are happening speedily, Esther seems to wait for the king to raise the issue of her request. By comparison with the banquet details in chapter 5, this seems to take quite a while. Certainly the wine is in full flow (verse 2). Esther is not impetuous, but patient. She works within the constraints which the king's position places on her.

Her accusation against the injustice awaiting her people comes in the guise of a request. It is emotionally charged, and the king is immediately aware of its critical nature. 'Grant me my life … spare my people' (verse 3). Her words are concise and personal. She cleverly arouses the king's attention by raising the possibility of his honoured queen losing her very life! His own words give her confidence: he had called her queen and had promised to do anything she wished (verse 2).

Her plea is supported by evidence. She repeats the verbs 'destroy', 'kill', 'annihilate', (verse 4), which feature in the decree Xerxes' had sealed (see 3:13). This must have made alarms bells ring in Xerxes' mind. The effect of recalling the decree is of course that Esther gives her background away. She obviously considers this a risk worth taking.

Esther is careful to assure Xerxes he is not to blame. Rather, she suggests that the blame lies with Haman (see 3:9; 4:7). She also appeals to Xerxes' sense of pride. She claims that if her problem was just about selling her people into slavery she wouldn't have thought it worthy of the king's attention. But this is a matter of life and death (verse 4).

Esther saves the most difficult thing till last. It is only in response to Xerxes' question that she reveals the identity of the culprit (verse 6). Briefly she describes him as 'vile', and says no more. It is as if she resists rubbing salt in the wound – or maybe she is simply petrified. The dilemma she has presented to Xerxes forces him to choose between Haman and his queen. But the tone of his words in verse 5 would have given Esther confidence: he sounds disgusted and keen to right the wrong.

The sentence of death

Verses 7–10 show us how the matter is resolved. The account has an ironic ring. Predictably, the king is enraged (verse 7), and because he seems unsure how to respond he relies on a nudge from one of his advisors again (verse 9). Esther plays no active part in the gruesome scene at all: she is protected from obvious blame. As for Haman, his punishment fits the crime:

► he feels the terror which he had previously inflicted upon the Jews (verse 6);

► he is accused, just as he had falsely accused the Jews (verse 8);

► he suffers loss of honour and the shame of disgrace (verse 8); and

► he is hanged on the gallows that he had erected for Mordecai (verses 9–10).

The final nail in his coffin is the king's decision to interpret Haman's pleas to Esther as inappropriate behaviour (verse 8). Far from obtaining mercy, Haman seals his own fate. The man who had become totally consumed by the fact that one Jewish man (Mordecai) wouldn't bow before him is now falling at the feet of one Jewish woman (Esther), begging for mercy. He is given no opportunity to defend himself; the former accuser is himself silenced. Haman's face is covered over (a custom that was common in judicial proceedings outside Persia too). This detail in verse 8 seems to symbolize disgrace, just as in 6:12. With Haman's hanging his downfall is complete. Now the scene is set for someone else to assume the honour which has been so conclusively stripped from him.

Questions

1. How far (if at all) does Xerxes redeem himself in this chapter? What does his example tell us about the way a leader's personality shapes his or her leadership style?
2. How would Esther's faith in her calling 'for such a time as this' (4:14) have been affected by this episode? Try to imagine her emotions through the events of this chapter. How does faith work with actions in the lives of God's people today? James 2:14–26 elaborates on this theme.
3. Should the punishment always fit the crime? (See, for example, Obadiah 15; Galatians 6:7.) Why or why not? What place is there for mercy in penal systems? How can we account for the fact that Esther is presented as blameless even though she didn't plead for mercy for Haman?

Esther 8:1–14

Honoured!

Esther and Mordecai take further steps to secure the future of the Jewish people. A new edict is speedily released, allowing the Jews to protect themselves.

 Sportsmen and women claim that there is no greater honour than playing for their country. They feel personal and corporate pride in their commitment to the team and its glory. In these verses Esther and Mordecai receive personal honour and achieve corporate honour for the Jewish people. It is impossible to miss the excitement in the story. Just as athletes need to stick to their training programme, so Esther and Mordecai are committed to the task. They cannot and do not get sidetracked. The honour they receive (verses 1–2) is simply a means to an end, and the end is now theirs for the grasping.

Honour is transferred

The shame suffered by Haman in chapter 7 contrasts with the honour given to Esther and Mordecai in verses 1–2. The contrast is made even more striking by the transfer of the symbols of Haman's previous honour to Mordecai and Esther.

First, *Esther receives Haman's 'estate'*. It was normal for a criminal's property to be transferred to the king, but Xerxes' decision to pass it on to Esther is unexpected. 'Estate' may include family as well as property. If so, Haman's entire legacy is put at Esther's disposal.

Secondly, *Mordecai receives Haman's status*. The phrase

135

'Mordecai came into the presence of the king' shows us that Mordecai is given the special privilege of entering the king's presence without a summons. Haman had exercised this privilege too (there is no indication that he was summoned in 3:8, for example).

Thirdly, *Mordecai receives Haman's ring.* The ring is an important symbol of the king's own authority, and had been given to Haman in order to seal the edict against the Jews (see 3:10, 12). The transfer of the ring is highly significant: Xerxes is virtually saying that the authority that was Haman's, to pass edicts in the king's name, has now passed to Mordecai. The king is placing his trust and his reputation in Mordecai's hands. Verse 2 adds that Esther too trusts Mordecai, appointing him over Haman's estate. She thus equips Mordecai to play his ongoing part in the victory of the Jews.

The writer hurries us through these events: the opening words of verse 1 indicate that Haman's demise is quickly balanced by Mordecai's rise. The words 'how he was related to her' (verse 1) are better translated 'what he meant to her'. Esther is telling the king about the nature and quality of her relationship with Mordecai, and that is why Xerxes confers further honour on him. It is as if the king is convinced that anyone closely connected with Esther must be good news for him.

Begging with honour

In verses 3–6 we see Esther's steadfast character. She may have money and position now, but her primary focus remains her people rather than herself. This sense of solidarity is a hallmark of the Jewish people throughout their history, for their faith is exercised in community. Esther retains a passionate sense of vocation. She falls down in supplication and weeps before the king (verse 3). She is totally committed to her people (verse 6). Her own well-being is nothing to her if they are under threat. Verse 5 even suggests that Esther still feels very threatened herself. Either she is nervous or she is overdoing the courtesy. Her bold request to Xerxes challenges him to do the almost impossible. She tries to show that the original edict was really all about Haman rather than about Xerxes. In effect she says, 'You can overrule this edict because it wasn't really yours in the first place.'

The king is obviously moved by Esther's heartfelt pleas (verse 4), but verses 7–8 suggest he feels impotent to change things. The force of these verses doesn't come over too well in some of our English versions. Xerxes' words almost accuse Esther: 'Look at all I've done already for you. I've done enough. The rest is up to you. If you want another decree, you write it!' He hands over responsibility to Esther and Mordecai. Thus the transfer of honour and power is complete. Just as Haman had organized the decree against the Jews, Mordecai organizes the writing and sending of the new decree.

Another decree sealed and sent out

Verses 9–14 mirror the words and order in 3:12–15. The differences arise from the changed circumstances surrounding the edicts and the people involved. Given the two-month delay since the publication of Haman's decree (as allowed by verse 9), the timing of Mordecai's decree is uncertain. The author may be primarily concerned with the speed of events now that Esther has secured permission from the king to get another decree in place. Verse 9 begins by suggesting that Mordecai didn't delay. The best and fastest horses are used: horses that represent the king's authority (verse 10).

The decree is summarized in verse 11. It allows the Jewish people the dignity and right to protect themselves against their attackers, and even to plunder them. If Mordecai had learnt anything from Haman, it seems to be how to publicize a decree; Mordecai follows Haman's procedure in this (verses 12–13).

As the edict is issued, the tables are being turned. The disaster the Jews face is quickly being averted.

Questions

1. How easy or difficult have you found it to follow God's plans when the going is tough? What about when things are easier? In what circumstances are you most likely to lose the sense of God's call on your life?
2. What do we learn here about friendship and loyalty? How do you feel about Esther's passionate commitment to her people? How can we develop such a care for God's people ourselves?
3. How do you (or should you) respond to the many wrongs that need to be righted in our world today? How can we come to terms with the spirit of verse 11, given Jesus' teaching about loving our enemies (see Matthew 5:43–44)?

Esther 8:15–17

In royal robes again

Mordecai's honour and the contents of the new edict are received with great joy and celebration.

The theme has changed from Haman's shame to Mordecai's honour. In these three verses that honour is coupled with celebration. There is something very attractive about celebration among God's people. In the Bible this is always the case. Whether it's the praise of individuals (expressed in song or prose, spontaneous or using set words) or the corporate celebration of God's people (for physical deliverance, daily provision or spiritual

blessings), it is always contagious. Take the beggar who
celebrated his restored sight. 'When all the people saw it,
they also praised God' (Luke 18:43). Take the celebration of
the early church: 'Everyone was filled with awe ... And the
Lord added to their number daily those who were being
saved' (Acts 2:43, 47). The Old Testament instructions
relating to feasts and festivals emphasize rejoicing and
celebration (see for example the instructions for the
Passover, the Feast of Weeks and the Feast of Tabernacles in
Deuteronomy 16). Such celebration not only gives rise to
blessing, but also acts as a testimony to those outside: 'Then
all the peoples on earth will see that you are called by the
name of the LORD, and they will fear you' (Deuteronomy
28:3–6, 10). All God's people are called to celebrate God's
work now and always. Celebration is a distinctive mark
of a grateful and obedient people, and invites others to
respond.

Crowned

Mordecai's honour is now real rather than staged and
symbolic (contrast the end of chapter 6). Chapter 6
anticipates his rise, which is realized now that Haman is
gone. Mordecai's new clothes are described in detail,
suggesting that they are important (verse 15). They are like
royal garments. Some of Xerxes' own authority is reflected
in Mordecai's crown and robe. We are given similar details
of Daniel's clothes when he is made third in command over
the Babylonian empire (Daniel 5:7, 29). Although the details
are not identical, the parallel suggests that Mordecai's
clothes show that he now stands alongside Xerxes and
Esther.

The colours of Mordecai's garments are interesting. Gold
and purple are particularly associated with the clothes of
priests (see, for example, Exodus 28:6). Throughout the
story, Mordecai has undertaken a priest-like function. He
speaks for the Jews as a whole and typifies their responses
(for example, 4:1, 13–14). Now this role is to be formally
recognized. The Jews rejoice because their representative,

who will continue to work on their behalf, has been elevated to a position of honour and authority. But it was the whole 'city of Susa' that held a 'joyous celebration' (verse 15): everyone, not just the Jews, realizes that Haman's demise and Mordecai's rise mean good news.

Celebrating

The writer uses four words to express the emotional celebrating of the Jewish people: 'happiness', 'joy', 'gladness' and 'honour' (verse 16). The first word is in fact 'light' (which is often used symbolically of the joy that contrasts with the darkness of despair; see, for example, Psalms 97:11; 112:4). Light dispels darkness, and this is what has happened. The four emotions mentioned here displace those described in 4:3: 'great mourning', 'fasting', 'weeping' and 'wailing' are things of the past.

Converting

In verse 17 it is almost as if the writer gets carried away with excitement. The celebration is clearly not just about Mordecai, but also about the publication of the new edict. It now infiltrates every province and city. Until now, Mordecai's influence has mirrored that which Haman had previously exercised: here it goes beyond it. No-one is exempt from the implications of this edict, which Mordecai has sealed in the name of the king. Even though the Jews' victory is not yet realized, it seems secure because other people begin to join their numbers. The meaning of 'became Jews' is debatable, but it certainly implies that there was a general feeling that it would be advantageous to be connected with the Jews in the future.

'Fear of the Jews' may mean that their numerical or military strength is now seen as a force to be reckoned with, especially now that the new edict has given them the right to defend themselves (verse 11). But perhaps the writer is hinting that this reversal of fortunes should convince people, including the reader, that God turns his favour

towards his people. Something has been going on under-
neath the surface events. Divine power has turned disaster
and dismay into jubilation and joy. No wonder everyone is
filled with awe! God has turned the situation around.

Questions

1. Have you experienced a reversal of fortunes which can
   only be explained in terms of God's intervention? What
   happened? Spend some time in celebration, praising God
   for what he did. Look for an opportunity to use your
   story in your witness to a non-Christian friend.
2. What characterizes celebration in praise of God? When
   you celebrate like this, how are you and those around
   you affected? What about when your church celebrates?
   How much celebration is there in your church's worship?
   If it is lacking, why?
3. How do you respond to people in authority? Why? What
   is the right attitude to authority in the church and in the
   state (see e.g. 1 Thessalonians 5:12–13; 1 Timothy 5:17;
   Romans 13:1–7; 1 Timothy 2:1–3; Titus 3:1–21)? How does
   this compare with attitudes you see around you in
   society?

5

CELEBRATE GOD'S VICTORY!

Esther 9 – 10

Stop and look

'Don't let it go to your head.' 'Win with grace and humility.' That's how we are usually advised to handle our successes. But there is little graciousness in chapter 9. Victory is secured in a rather callous and merciless fashion. The people take no risks. They do not hesitate or hold back. Once victory is secured, they celebrate unashamedly and repeatedly. The message is loud and clear: only complete victory will do, and only extremes of celebration are appropriate. The colossal scale of the victory celebrations emphasizes how serious the battle had been. Haman (and by implication his family also) were nothing less than the enemy of God's people. And the enemy of God's people is nothing less than the opponent of God himself. In God's eternal purposes his enemies will be totally defeated. The Purim festival celebrates that defeat. It serves as a lasting invitation to us all to participate in and celebrate God's eternal purposes, even in a world where his presence is at times unseen.

Purim is the lasting legacy of the story of Esther. Because she decided to co-operate with God's plan, the course of history was changed to fulfil his eternal purposes. The book of Esther presents each of us with a personal challenge: do we co-operate with God's purposes in a world where his presence is unrecognized but so vital? But Esther's story also presents us with a corporate challenge: do we stand together as God's people to defeat God's enemies, to secure God's purposes, to celebrate his victory achieved for us? If we do, the course of history may be changed through us, and the world will celebrate with us as God's interaction with human lives is revealed.

'The tables were turned'

The crisis is resolved, and the Jews celebrate their victory over their enemies.

Through involvement with my local church, I have recently been reminded that expecting God to work is one thing; experiencing his working is something else. We have been expecting God to do something new among us and now we are beginning to experience his work and enjoy it. In Esther 9, what the Jews had already expected and rejoiced about actually happens. As a result, their lives as God's people are changed for ever – a new festival of celebration takes its place in their calendars. The movement from expectancy to experience and from experience to celebration is a common biblical pattern repeated in the lives of God's people throughout the centuries. It reminds us that God's work is always in progress, and that our participation and response are always required.

The chapter begins by simply explaining that the Jews have the advantage over their enemies because

▶ other nationalities are afraid of them (verse 2);

▶ all sorts of officials help them (verse 3); and

▶ Mordecai is prominent and powerful (verse 4).

The chapter then gives details about the defeat of their enemies:

▶ the Jews are free to do what they want to their enemies (verse 5);

- in the palace at Susa they kill 500 men plus the ten sons of Haman on 13 Adar (verse 6);
- in Susa as a whole they kill another 300 men on 14 Adar (verse 15); and
- in the provinces they kill 75,000 men (verse 16).

Amid the numerical details two particular aspects are emphasized:

- the Jews do not touch their enemies' plunder (verses 10, 15–16); and
- the timing of the stages of the defeats is significant (13 and 14 Adar).

It is difficult to isolate the main purpose of chapters 9 – 10. It is as if the writer is trying to achieve a number of things all at once. The crisis for the Jews needs to be resolved. The story must be brought to a conclusion. But at the same time the portrayal of the characters of Esther and Mordecai needs to be completed, and the threat represented by Haman has to be fully laid to rest. In addition, the first nineteen verses prepare for the chapter's second part: the story of Esther is not significant just in its own time, but leaves a lasting legacy. So chapter 9 begins to draw the story to a close and to explain that lasting legacy.

The enemies' plans are reversed

There's nothing quite so disturbing as the unexpected. Even when it is good news, it can disturb our plans, our priorities, our perspectives. Verse 1 anticipates the positive conclusion of the story, but still reminds us that there is something seemingly impossible about that conclusion. The verse recalls Haman's edict. The exact date of its implementation has now arrived (compare 3:13). The Jews have wept and fasted and mourned about this day, but now they dare (with us) to expect the unexpected because 'the tables are turned'. Now 13 Adar means that not one edict but two are due to be implemented; the plans of Haman and Mordecai collide. We have already been told that the Jews now had the upper hand because other people were afraid of them (8:17), and verse 2 emphasizes this point again. As the royal officials and governors become mere assistants to the Jews (verse 3), Mordecai grows in pre-eminence (verse 4). These details intensify the idea that the reversal is complete at every level. The honour Mordecai assumes requires others besides Haman to take a drop in status.

Those who now face destruction at the hands of the Jews are pointedly (and repeatedly) identified as 'those who hated them' and 'their enemies' (verses 1, 5). Although the Jews were able to do 'what they pleased' (verse 5), and the details of the edict itself suggest they had a free hand, they work within limits (8:11).

What turned tables look like

The numbers recorded in verses 7–16 suggest at least one thing: the mass destruction of the Jews that Haman had planned was matched by the mass destruction of the Jews' enemies. The exact figures seem less important than this general point. The Jews inflict massive losses on their opponents.

These verses make the slaughter of Haman's family central: all his sons are killed, and are publicly disgraced as their corpses are hung on gallows (verse 14). These details do away with Haman's legacy, stripping his memory of the honour of having many sons (a fact he had boasted about in 5:11). But there may be a further point here: the Jews had committed themselves to eliminate the Amalekites (whom Haman represents in this story, see comments on 3:1–6; see also Exodus 17:8–16; Deuteronomy 25:17–19). Esther's request to bring utter disgrace upon Haman's family can, then, be interpreted as an expression of her commitment to God's purposes regarding the Amalekites.

Three times it is noted that the Jews didn't take the plunder from their enemies (verses 10, 15–16). Taking plunder is in fact permitted by the decree (see 8:11), but by choosing not to do so the Jews bring to mind their own history whereby accepting the spoil of a defeated enemy had become unacceptable (Genesis 14:21–23; 1 Samuel 15). Perhaps the concern here is to protect the Jews from blame. The destruction of their enemies is not about filling their pockets, but about their preservation as the community of God's people.

Esther's part in extending the destruction of her people's enemies for another day (verse 13) has often caused concern. Where is the reticent woman we met at the start of the story? She certainly has no loss of nerve here! The part she plays is significant:

▶ she is responsible for the final disgrace of Haman's sons, and in this way fulfils her vocation, which has a long-term as well as an immediate effect;

▶ the two-day celebration of Purim is directly connected to her;

▶ her favour with the king has been a theme throughout the story, and so the fact that she makes this bold request emphasizes her status as heroine of the story.

What turned tables feel like

Verses 17–19 explain why the celebration of the Purim festival was not uniform. The Jews in the provinces fought their enemies on one day and celebrated on the next (verses 16–17), whereas those in Susa fought for two days and celebrated on the third (verses 15, 18).

These verses capture what such a dramatic reversal of outcome feels like for God's people. Joyful feasting breaks out everywhere. Even the feasting in the Persian palace (described in chapter 1) did not match this kind of joy and feasting. It is also significant that the Jews rested (verses 17–18). In other words, this day feels like a Sabbath. Their trouble is now gone and there is peace and security amid the joy and feasting. Presents are exchanged, expressing a generous, happy and united spirit among God's people.

The significance is clear. God's people are preserved, but, more than that, their victory over their enemies is complete. The impact of this is to change their life together for ever.

Questions

1. What 'enemies' do Christians have? (Think of the forces and pressures, inside us as well as outside, that oppose our living for God.) Are we sufficiently ruthless in dealing with them? If not, why not?
2. Is it important for the church to hold special festivals? Why or why not? What are the benefits? What are the pitfalls?
3. Which principles in this chapter can be applied to oppressive situations in the world today? When, if ever, is it justifiable to use violence in order to right wrongs?

Esther 9:20–32

Purim: a festival to celebrate salvation

Purim is officially adopted as a new annual festival to celebrate the story of Esther.

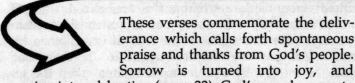 These verses commemorate the deliverance which calls forth spontaneous praise and thanks from God's people. Sorrow is turned into joy, and mourning into celebration (verse 22). God's people agree to remember his deliverance for ever, wherever they may find themselves (verse 28). There is a great sense of commitment

and excitement. We are reminded of prophetic passages like Isaiah 61, which celebrates the reversal of fortunes which God's people experience on the day of salvation. The terminology is similar: captives will know freedom, prisoners will experience release, mourners will know gladness, and the despairing will praise God (Isaiah 61:1–3).

Purim is instituted

Mordecai sends letters to all the Jews in Xerxes' kingdom, encouraging them to hold a festival for two days each year. Specifically, the Jews are told to celebrate because

▶ they have experienced 'relief' from their enemies;

▶ they are now left alone and free from danger; and

▶ their sorrow and mourning have turned into joy and new life.

Mordecai also instructs them to give presents of food to one another and to the poor. These acts of generosity reflect common themes in Jewish celebration: they must remember the less fortunate and express the community which brings all God's people together. In the story, God's people go together through the experience of despair. By giving gifts to one another, they now share in and increase one another's joy.

Purim is adopted

Mordecai's instructions are carried out (verses 23–28). The initially spontaneous celebrations are formalized. This is not to be a one-off celebration, but an established custom (verses 27–28). The name of the festival is explained by a brief retelling of the story (verses 24–26). It is associated with the lot cast by Haman to determine when the Jews should be destroyed (3:7). Purim therefore centres on the overthrow of the influence of this action. The importance of celebrating this reversal is emphasized by the repeated use of 'every' and 'all' in verses 27–28. Once again, the Jews expect other people to join them in their celebrations (verse 27). There is indeed something attractive about God's people together celebrating his work among them.

Purim is confirmed

Esther has not been mentioned since 9:13, where she saw off the legacy of Haman and his family. She reappears in verses 29–32 to confirm and verify the details of the Purim festival. The writer obviously wants his readers to support the festival. He confirms its importance in several ways:

▶ the Jewish population didn't have to be told to celebrate, it happened spontaneously and felt right to them (verse 18);

▶ Mordecai confirmed that it was appropriate and important (verse 22);

▶ the Jewish people together agreed that they should continue to celebrate the festival (verses 23, 27);

▶ Esther – Queen Esther, no less – confirms Purim (verses 29, 32);

▶ Mordecai and Esther are at one on this (verse 31); and

▶ Esther's decree about Purim is written down in the records (verse 32).

The result is that the festival of Purim is set up to last longer than the Persian court itself. What is written down about Purim are words of 'peace and truth' (verse 30, literally; 'goodwill and assurance' in the NIV). These terms could describe the content of Esther and Mordecai's letter, but equally might characterize its results. The point may be that Purim would establish peace and truth. As peace and truth are marks of God's work, celebrating Purim is nothing less than co-operating with God.

Questions

1. Esther writes 'with full authority' (verse 29). How and why have Esther's personality and vocation been transformed in this story? How might your life be similarly transformed?
2. In your life together as God's people, how much do generosity and care for the poor characterize your church? If they are lacking, why? Why do these characteristics amount to co-operating with God?
3. Which festivals attract attention in the world today? Why? How might Christian festivals play a part in mission to the world?

The Purim festival today

Today, Jews observe the festival of Purim at the end of a day of fasting (the Fast of Esther). Each family holds a banquet, with fun and dancing. Gifts of food are exchanged between friends and given to the poor. Children dress up as the main characters: royal Mordecai, beautiful Esther, evil Haman. As the story of Esther is retold, they make a lot of noise with shakers and other instruments every time the name of Haman is mentioned. The role of the children emphasizes that Esther, though a young girl, played an important part in destroying Israel's enemies. As they 'boo' Haman, they oppose their peoples' enemies and usher in the new future which the festival celebrates.

Life goes on

The accomplishments of Xerxes and Mordecai are recorded.

I recently spoke to a neighbour who is grieving the death of her daughter. 'Life goes on,' she said. 'We must start getting back to normal.' These last verses of the story of Esther remind us that life goes on. We started in chapter 1 with life in the Persian Empire and we end in chapter 10 with the same empire. In the intervening chapters, we have lived through a crisis for the Jews. Now that it has been averted, life goes on. But the life that goes on is different from the life that had gone before. Things have changed; the tables have been turned and remain turned. Life after experiencing God's deliverance and intervention in a crisis situation will not be the same as life before it.

Life is different

First of all, *life is different for Xerxes*. He still has a large empire, but now he takes the initiative in its organization. 'He imposed tribute' (verse 1). Whether this was a monetary tax or forced labour, at least he is now exercising royal authority. The early chapters suggest that he did little apart from giving banquets to celebrate his own wealth and majesty (1:4). Here the emphasis is on his power and might rather than on his wealth (10:2). There is something more honourable about his kingship now, and this has to do with his new second-in-command.

Secondly, *life is different for Mordecai*. He is no longer just sitting at the king's gate. He himself is great, and second-in-command to Xerxes alone. He has assumed Haman's position. More than that, his 'acts of power and might' are written in the book of the annals of the kings ...' The use of this phrase puts Mordecai on a par with the kings of Judah and Israel (see, for example, 1 Kings 11:41). Mordecai is held in high esteem by the king as well as by the people. This is very different from the scorn which he had previously suffered from Haman.

Thirdly, *life is very, very different for the Jewish people*. They now have a friend in high places rather than an enemy. Mordecai is committed to their welfare. The last phrase of verse 3 could be translated: 'He was seeking the good of his people and was speaking peace for all their descendants.' This indicates that he is concerned for the long-term good of the Jewish people, not just their immediate welfare. The word for 'peace' (*shalom*) refers to physical, emotional, social and spiritual well-being. It describes life that is positively good, not just without conflict.

Life goes on after the crisis caused by Haman, but things are now different. The day of death has passed and now God's people can live. This is the Bible's message of salvation. It can be experienced in the here and now even when God seems absent. But it will be fully realized in the age to come, when God will be forever present and visible.

Even today God's people have a friend in high places. He is our security and our peace, for he destroys the wall that divides enemies, thus making peace (Ephesians 2:14–15). God's people live transformed lives. We have encountered God's providence and grace. What a reason to celebrate, to praise and to live!

Questions

1. How has your life been changed by your encounter with God? What have you discovered about him through times of crisis and difficulty?
2. Who are the people in our world today who speak up for the rights of others? How can we support their work and

increase their influence? What part should the church (local and on a wider scale) play in this?

3. What has the book of Esther taught you? What might God be saying to you about his call on your life and your service in the church and in the world? What response do you need to make to what you have discovered?

For further reading

David Atkinson, *The Message of Ruth* (IVP, 1983)
Joyce Baldwin, *Esther: An Introduction and Commentary* (IVP, 1984)
Frederic Bush, *Ruth and Esther* (Word, 1996)
Robert Hubbard, *The Book of Ruth* (Eerdmans, 1988)
Karen Jobes, *Esther* (Zondervan, 1999)